Political Government

Political Government

Robert Klassen
With Contributions by Alvin Lowi, Jr.

Writers Club Press
New York Lincoln Shanghai

Political Government

Writers Club Press
an imprint of iUniverse, Inc.

For information address:
iUniverse
2021 Pine Lake Road, Suite 100
Lincoln, NE 68512
www.iuniverse.com

ISBN: 0-595-25811-5

Printed in the United States of America

This is written for Homo Sapiens once again, in the fond hope that we will grow up before it's too late.

ACKNOWLEDGEMENTS

First, I would like to thank Alvin Lowi, Jr., for his invaluable kindness, instruction, and advice, and for contributing two of his fine essays to this book. Next, I would like to thank Lew Rockwell for publishing most of my essays on his premier individualist libertarian web site, www.lewrockwell.com. Finally, I would like to thank Susan Mickelberry, a professional editor at the University of Florida, for her keen criticism of both my thinking and my writing.

PREFACE

I have departed from traditional attribution of sources here, i.e. footnotes, since nearly all of my research was done on the Internet. Therefore I am including the original URLs in this paper and ink copy of the various essays that were written for Internet publication. We'll see how that endures over time.

INTRODUCTION

This publication marks the end of my foray into criticism of political government. It is intended to be a companion volume to *Economic Government,* examining the opposite side of the coin in more detail. What is political government, and how does it differ from economic government?

From Random House Dictionary (1978):

"Political, adj., of or involved in politics or government."

"Politics, n., the art or science of government."

"Government, n., the political direction and control exercised over a nation, state, community, etc."

Rather circular definitions, this dictionary points to the problem of the words, political and government, assumed to be the same thing. So let's go back to the word, govern: "1. to rule by right of authority, 2. to exercise a directing influence over."

I would distinguish between two different kinds of government.

Political government is any set of institutions which rule mankind by assumed right of authority. The key word here is rule, that is giving orders backed by the threat of force.

Economic government is any set of institutions which influence mankind by free choice of individuals. The key word here is influence, that is to produce a desired result without the threat of force.

For example, the hospital where I work employs two-thousand people, not a single one of whom comes to work stinking and dirty. Why is that? There is no political law against being dirty, or legal threat of force for stinking, but there is powerful peer influence in a hospital to be clean and odor free. That influence applies only to employees, who might be sent home by a supervisor to get cleaned up, for in fact hospital patients are often dirty and stinking and they are still admitted. This example serves to demonstrate that selective influence works.

Mankind in general disparages the use of force or fraud in moral proscriptions against lying, cheating, stealing, and killing, yet there are always defectors from these common social mores whose behavior must be curtailed if society is to proceed in peace and harmony. Political government is supposedly established to do the curtailing, although in fact political government always becomes the biggest defector of all. Economic government would curtail the defectors by denying them a place in the economic life of society until they voluntarily and literally pay for their crimes. The primary institutions required to achieve this are insurance and banking, both of which have been thoroughly absorbed into political government. Despite this discouraging fact of contemporary life, a careful distinction between the two forms of government must still be made in order to isolate the totally different means of curtailing criminal activity, by force, or by influence, so that mankind may one day escape from the continual boom and bust cycle of politically founded civilizations.

CONTENTS

Mankind Versus The State

2001

Pretend this is a movie. We see a jungle path in the early morning twilight. An animal runs past, we can't quite make out what it is. Then a naked man appears, his skin painted in designs. He carries a blow-gun. Then another one appears, carrying a bow and arrow. Altogether, six painted men sneak down the path. Are they hunting the animal?

The scene switches to another jungle path, down which six naked men are running, shouting, and laughing. They also carry weapons, but their skins are not painted. Two men carry a dead animal tied to a spear.

Suddenly, a painted man jumps into the path, levels his blow-gun, and fires a poisoned dart into the back of an unpainted man. That man falls to the ground and all of the other men flee.

Now it is night. We see men dancing around a fire, celebrating a victory. Their stick and mud huts are in shadow, but we also see women and children huddled there, cheering the men on. We switch to another village, where men also dance around a fire, shouting in rage. The women and children are wailing. What do you suppose will happen next?

Please note, everybody in this story is under the age of thirty-five; the majority are teen-agers. For evidence of the truth of this scenario, I would first refer the reader to Homer, then query any search engine on primitive culture.

Mankind has its roots in this kind of social organization. Bands of a dozen up to four-dozen people lived in temporary camps and eked out a living from whatever plant and animal food happened to be available in their region. When the food supply ran low, they moved on. The use of physical force to get food and to retain control of food producing territory was, and still is among living hunter-gatherer tribes today, unremitting. Personally, I believe that the use of force to get what we want is natural to mankind and is, possibly, hard-wired into our nervous system. Today, however, this natural tendency may bring mankind to self-extinction, thanks to the modern political state.

The origin of the political state remains hidden in unrecorded history. There are many hypotheses, but the one that makes sense to me would place the beginning in the early agricultural revolution, when food supplies began to stabilize and people didn't need to move around as much. This would tally with archeological discoveries at Susa, Jericho, and Troy, possibly the first city-states in history. In Homer we find early city-states vying for regional dominance, although appearing not much different in organization from bands of hunter-gatherers, repeating the ancient pattern of human social behavior. By the time we get to the battle at Marathon in 490 B.C., the political state is an established human institution and its monopoly on the use of force is set in tradition for all time to come.

I think the time has come for us to examine the validity of the political state as a conceptual model for the organization of human society. One could argue that the state is valid as an historical precedent, that is, there has never been an alternative that worked. One could argue that the monopolization of force by the political state is necessary to prevent violent social chaos, or a reversion to the hunter-gatherer example of social behavior in my opening scenario. Or one could argue that only the political state can provide security and justice in human society. I think these arguments are specious and false.

The alternative model of human organization has been maturing before our eyes for two centuries. It is the private business corporation designed to create and sell products for a profit without the use of force. Academicians in favor of the state have recognized the potential threat of the corporation model to their cherished traditions since Karl Marx. Thanks largely to them, the corporation model of government has been throttled by the state monopoly on force from the outset.

Political state apologists of all stripes have described the private business corporation as the source of violent social chaos since the late Nineteenth Century. In verifiable fact, this is a lie. The true source of violent social chaos has always been, and still is, the state and its monopoly on the use of force.

Throttled private corporations have provided security and justice to whatever limited extent they were permitted by the state from their beginnings. Although researching or even thinking about insurance and banking corporations apart from state rules and regulations is nearly impossible, considering the potential of these private corporations is not impossible. Insurance and banking could provide the kind of security and justice people demand if they were allowed to do so (like making theft prohibitively expensive to the thief).

Now that Western Civilization and its respected social institutions have been attacked by Dark Age prophets and their henchmen, we are menaced once more by the foremost argument in favor of the state, total war. Who can imagine private corporations in the 21st Century protecting us from murderers out of the 10th Century? I can. Our private corporation airline personnel were disarmed by our state. They still are. I believe that private airlines could have done better without the state. But instead of secure private defense, we rely on our 21st Century state to bomb a 10th Century country into the Stone Age. I don't believe that total war is necessary or desirable to anybody except to the state.

Mankind's worldwide reaction to the WTC attack was twofold: some people danced around the campfire in celebration and some people danced around the campfire in rage. These reactions are natural to our species and so is the glower of hatred we express toward our enemies, whoever they may be at the moment. The state thrives on this reaction. But if we allow our states to escalate this posturing to the level of nuclear holocaust, then the survival of our species becomes at risk once more. As some members of my generation may recall, that was the issue throughout the Cold War. Now what?

Who would put Space Age technology into the hands of Dark Age warriors? Who armed these primitives? Who provoked them? The short-term imperatives of political governments always defeat the long-term intentions of civilization. Why do we endure this nonsense?

First, because it's a habit. The political state model for human social organization has been around forever, while the private corporation model has only been recognized as a viable alternative within the last fifty years. Second, because human technology has changed everything except human nature. Thanks to technology, human living conditions in the civilized world have never been this good, while political government has never been this dangerous to the survival of our species. Third, because the desire to use force for whatever reason that appeals to us at the moment lies deep within every human person. We dance around this fire.

Human nature might change in three or four million years of living in different circumstances, but it isn't going to change soon enough for us to avoid the collision that clearly lies ahead between our Space-Age technology and our Dark-Age philosophy of government. We must somehow find a way to make the use of force unprofitable, undesirable, and unthinkable to individual people and to our institutions of social organization, security, and justice. The private corporation model of government could do just that.

For further information about the corporation model of government, please read:

Citadel, Market, and Altar, by Spencer Heath, Yale University Press, 1957. Although out of print, this book may be available at: http://www.wepin.com/why/products/cmaa/cmaa.html

The Art of Community, by Spencer Heath MacCallum, Institute for Humane Studies, 1970. This book is available at: http://www.laissezfaire-books.com.

The Market For Liberty, by Linda and Morris Tannehill, Fox and Wilkes, 1993, original copyright 1970. This book is available at: http://www.laissezfairebooks.com.

The Discovery of Freedom, by Rose Wilder Lane, Fiftieth Anniversary Edition, Fox and Wilkes, 1993. This book is available at: http://www.laissezfairebooks.com.

Democracy, The God That Failed, by Hans-Hermann Hoppe, Transaction Publishers, 2001. This book is available at: http://www.lewrockwell.com.

Sic Itur ad Astra, by Andrew J. Galambos, The Universal Scientific Publications Company, 1999. This book is available at: http://www.laissezfairebooks.com.

Atlantis: A Novel about Economic Government, by Robert Klassen, Writers' Club Press, 1997. This book is available at: http://www.amazon.com.

A Natural History Of Paternalism And A Working Hypothesis For The Origin Of The State

Alvin Lowi, Jr.

December 27, 1998

You probably rankled under parental authority. I certainly did. I observe most people do if they live to maturity. If you have children, no doubt you are even more familiar with the pattern. It is probably a perpetual state of affairs.

However, where would you be now without your parents? Nowhere! First to be conceived, then born. Without some protection and cultivation from them, chances are you would not have matured into the person you are now, fulfilling at least a fraction of your potential, perhaps even more than your parents could have ever dreamed.

Trouble is, we all outgrow parental authority and vision. Not that we come to regard our parents with contempt, although this is known to happen on occasion. Most of us honor our fathers and mothers and even love them dearly throughout our lives, just like it says in the commandments.

7

Nevertheless, in all likelihood, there will come a time in the course of growing to maturity when we become restive and skeptical of our parents authority and wisdom.

Parents who face the "rebellion" of their children squarely and realistically are able to relax at some point and let their children go. In doing so, they will have earned the love and respect they get from their offspring. If they live long enough, either the parents or the offspring, they may eventually come to agreement on the ways of the world to live and let live.

Regardless, there remain some even more fundamental factors at work in the human psyche. Underlying all the esthetic, ethical, familial and biological connections that can be expressed by autonomous persons are some visceral attachments to our origins and our ancestors almost like the vestigial umbilical cord discarded at birth. One manifestation of this bond is a lingering nostalgia for the "good old days" in the womb and the family nest. Although there is no way for us to go back to such a state, we still carry a longing for such protection, comfort and security. No doubt, such longing is stronger in some than others.

Another manifestation is a sense of charity like being kind to babies and dumb animals. So if there is a longing for perpetual childhood, it should not be surprising to find some people with an inclination to play the counterpart, namely everlasting parenthood. If so, in due time, some assertive, perceptive and perhaps well-intended folks will recognize this generic fetal craving and regard it as an opportunity to shepherd the flock of mankind. Could be that the paternity-minded among us are called by their humanitarian instincts to spread the protective blanket of paternalistic statehood over everyone's continuing existence to satisfy what they believe is a universal quest for refuge from the cold cruel world outside the womb.

Unfortunately for mankind, a state catering to stereotyped dreams of perpetual childhood is irrelevant to human life in the real world. It dotes on an irrelevant vestige of biological history and tries to mimic natural parenthood, the only kind that is essential for the species and the kind that is naturally outgrown by individuals of the species. So parenthood is to society like tonsils and appendices are to the body. It becomes superfluous with maturity. Also like tonsils and appendices, parenthood lingering beyond biological and social necessity becomes vulnerable to infection and infirmity—At this point, parenthood becomes dysfunctional or even pathological.

Sociologists have long known that dysfunctional parenthood is a factor in the development of criminality and other sociopathic behavior. Political scientists might consider the analogous dysfunctionality in paternalistic government to be a factor in the occurrence of violence, sloth and poverty in the population.

The synthetic state of perpetual parenthood is applicable to mature, whole human individuals only by accident. Most adult humans will have outgrown parental dependency. So to re-institute parenthood by political means can only exacerbate and perpetuate the parental rankling phenomenon. The "papa" state, unable to "let go," thereby creates a waste of human resources though animosity and strife. These symptoms of social disease are attributable to dysfunctional parenthood of the synthetic variety.

Nowadays, most people recognize the papa or nanny state is not so much for them but for anonymous others. Rather, they excuse it on the basis that somebody must take care of all those down-and-out people on the street shunned by their kinfolk and neighbors and seemingly unable to take care of themselves. Controversy persists as to how those unfortunate people became so marginalized, alienated and vulnerable to circumstances in the first place (if they really are), or how they became invisible to common spontaneous charity on a person-to-person basis. Although genetics is a possible cause, chances are that most of the indigence and rejection of common humanity in evidence is traceable to dysfunctionalities in the synthetic parenthood of the state. Regardless, the occasional lapses of human dignity are extrapolated to humanity as a whole and attributed to a defective human nature. Thereby, the imposition of a state of perpetual parenthood over all is justified. Although this proposition is at stark odds with reality, it stands largely unchallenged.

No doubt there is broad support for the papa state notwithstanding the fact that the overwhelming number of its supporters are the very people who will never qualify to receive any of its purported beneficence. So how is it that so many people become so attached to a pure abstraction that has never proven to be workable for its intended purpose? The wealth of historical evidence points to the paternalistic state as the greatest cause of human destitution in the world. The cause and effect seems so tight that one might well wonder whether the architects of such a state could have an interest in destitution.

Perhaps people's susceptibility to this scheme of statehood and subjecthood arises from a vicarious experience of suffering the plight of the "poorer than them," real or hypothetical. Although poverty is real enough, it also serves as a reminder to the prosperous that there, but for the grace of God or papa state, go they. And then, the primitive longing for the warmth of the womb surfaces. If so, they might well crave to have the very idea of misfortune removed from their sight if only as an environmental clean-up measure. Such motivation could explain people's willingness to pay a ransom to anyone who claims to be able to rid them of such an affront to their humanitarian sensibilities. However, theirs is a false hope.

Perhaps the very thought of any misfortune in the world brings with it an unreasoned sense of guilt for good fortune. Then, the parental opportunists are poised and ready to assuage these guilt feelings among their fellows in anticipation of unending gratitude for the grace of the state they propose to perfect. Since there is no redemption for original sin—and feelings of guilt for ones virtues is such a sin—the papa state fails to quell such remorse. Does this discourage the surrogate papas? No indeed! It encourages them to persevere to even greater heights of paternalism.

The would-be papa glories in his worshipful flock, especially those sympathetic sufferers among them who subscribe to his grandiloquent and seemingly magnanimous gestures. Some of his supporters may be gratified by a vicarious sense of charity in supporting the scheme. However, most are merely shamed or intimidated into compliance by their more righteously motivated peers. Only rarely does it occur to any of them that there is nothing charitable about a scheme to forcibly redistribute the wealth of their fellow man. To impoverish all to some degree by force in order to remedy the plight of a few may sound charitable until the actual distribution of the take is accounted for. Only then is it recognizable that the principal need being served by this scheme is papa's own. How he manages to prey on most people's sense of fairness to get them to foot his bills with no questions asked is a rather remarkable accomplishment and a historical curiosity.

Meanwhile, regardless of sentiments to the contrary, most of us succeed in fleeing the coop. We do so to further our own lives in the realization that our own initiative is our best hope for a life after birth. Not that we escape certain indentures and impostures imposed on us by the chicken master and his henchmen for the duration of their tenure. But we generally rejoice in the residue of freedom available to us regardless of guilt. We may even celebrate our good fortune with generous material gestures of charity toward others less fortunate.

In the uninhibited and risk-laden world outside the coop, we make our lives our own in spontaneous society among like-minded adult individuals. Whereupon, we manage to produce the sustenance for a continuation of our lives in particular and human life in general. We may even become papas and mamas in our own right thereby continuing the cycle. We strive for life beyond procreative necessity. Were this not so, our species would have become extinct before it started. Perpetual parenthood has never been relevant to this historical event.

Curiously, it is only possible for the surrogate papa, mama or nanny state to masquerade as it does because of the antecedence and growth of autonomous human activity. Conceivably, this is the genie escaped from the bottle, never to be returned no matter what the shepherds of state and their functionaries would try to accomplish with their political institutions. Indeed, nowadays, autonomy is given a long leash by the statists as the best means to meet their economic ends. They have come around to the realization that perpetual children are perpetual dependents who eat the bacon but don't produce it or bring it home to papa.

In times past, the paternal masquerade took on a more literally familial form. A king or queen assumed the position of head of the "family" flock by divine right in mimicry of the natural nuclear family. Indeed, there was often an inherited blood or tribal connection that could not be broken even by violence. History cannot be denied. There are a few cases where aristocratic family rulership was ended by assassination to be replaced by a military dictatorship as in France and China, or a dictatorship of the so-called proletariat (the party) as in Russia and again in China. Since millions perished in the aftermath in each instance, the revolutionary reactions to the Bourbons, Romanovs, Mandarins and such can hardly qualify as either humane or progressive. But they do appear to be related to the vestigial rebellion against parental authority of the kind that cannot let go.

The American Revolution brought a new, ostensibly non-violent, form to this masquerade. The writer of the Declaration of Independence recognized that human individuality was inclined to rebel against parental authority of any kind and gave vent to the phenomenon. Subsequently, the founders of the republic closed this vent with The Constitution of 1787, once again instituting a synthetic state of order according to parental custom. In doing so, they resurrected an old form of statecraft invented by the ancient Greeks (Plato) to fill a perceived vacuum left by the banishment from the shores of the new world the even older monarchical ritual. This "new" ritual, now known as democratic politics, seemed at the time to be a better fit with the pantheistic and egalitarian ideas of the founders. They rejected the prosaic notion of a personal or anthropomorphic papa of all. Their new "democratic" political state, which they called a republic, would obscure an underlying aristocracy with superficial universality and a contrived competition for control of the social apparatus of coercion. Where formerly politics was strictly a palace game of intrigue and violence in which there was a loser for every winner (see Machiavelli), the American experiment opened access to those shenanigans to the people at large. However, this so-called democratic development did not change the nature of the game. In retaining a monopoly state, the founders continued the traditional zero-sum contest for supremacy to control state authority. A new non-hereditary aristocracy would soon discover the power of the paternalistic program and the rest is history.

Had it not been for the sheer political ineptitude of this American democratic contrivance, the humane visions of the founders might never have been realized. The demise of the old order was accompanied by an interregnum in North America that continued for a time due to political incompetence. In the temporary absence of state paternalism, autonomous human activity expanded and brought with it a spontaneous kind of order rarely seen in the world before, at least not on the scale now manifest. This was the outcome that attracted the oppressed multitudes from the old world to flee their respective coops to try and realize their dreams for a humane future. This inadvertent occurrence would eventually expose all the absurdities of the papa state for future generations to ridicule and eventually to ignore.

Unfortunately, this new "democracy" would leave nameless the reality of spontaneous self-rule in the marketplace that could give the word democracy some real meaning. Nevertheless as a result, we now have experience and visibility as to how human life actually persists and progresses without perpetual bondage to parenthood of any kind. In this apparently natural uprising of humanity we find a truly universal and humane system that goes on quite nicely in spite of political detractions and no name. This phenomenon is the inspiration for "America the Beautiful." The United States of America and its splendid political pageant is something else entirely.

Bad Habits

2002

Years ago, a respected colleague told me that she was watching hard-core pornographic movies in her psychology class at the university. I was shocked. Why would a church member, a happily married mother of three, a nursing supervisor be watching such evil garbage? Why would a university sponsor such a thing? The purpose, she said, was to desensitize candidates for a Masters Degree in Public Health to the seamy side of society. They would be exposed to worse and they had to be able to cope with it in a reasonable manner.

I got to thinking about that. How many things am I insensitive to? Driving a car, for one. Here I am sitting in an insulated and air-conditioned steel box hurtling down the road at seventy miles per hour. I don't feel any sensation of moving at that speed. I listen to music. I am not afraid. But I should be afraid. My nervous system is not constructed to respond to danger at that speed. During the Nineteenth Century, people on trains were terrified of moving at twenty miles per hour. But they got used to it. Me too. I acquired the habit of driving.

How about income taxes? That was a shocker to the folks who got hit with it for the first time. Many fled the country. But for most of us today, the income tax is a painless deduction from our paycheck. When we calculate our consumption needs, we don't even bother to think about the deductions, we think about what we've got left. It's become a habit.

What about so-called defense spending. Of course we don't think about that, we have no control over it. We don't see our income winging its way to Washington and we don't see what Washington does with it. They talk in billions, we think in thousands, or hundreds, or twenties. How can defense spending mean anything to us? So we ignore it, out of habit.

Are we sensitive to killing? Now I had some first-hand experience at killing steers and chickens and pigs as a farm boy, so I know how it's done. I've never killed another human being, however, although in my profession I've witnessed thousands of deaths. I suppose there are a fair number of Americans who have had first-hand experience at killing human beings; I can't imagine how they might feel about that. I wonder how people overall feel about killing human beings?

We see killing every day on television drama. We hear about killing every day from the media. Some government flunky, or thug, preaches at us about the killing rules of the day, every day. Yet, for us common folks, the rule is: Thou Shalt Not Kill. And we don't. Somebody else does. Are we sensitive to that?

I don't think so. For how many generations have the American people been forced into orgies of killing by the State? I count five. One generation's experience has been passed to the next with heroic rituals! Flags wave and trumpets sound: We slaughtered them! And the children march with toy guns. Until they grow up, when they march with real guns. Then some sanctimonious State hypocrite announces a new target for killing on television, only this time it's US. We sit numb. No, we are not sensitive to killing.

Let's break this vicious habit.

Previously published at http://www.lewrockwell.com

AMERICAN GULAG

A Story

2002

I heard them coming, of course, you can hear everything that happens from inside a small travel trailer at three in the morning. Their ritual, that's all. If they wanted to surprise me, they should have come at three in the afternoon, when the A/C was running. Too public, maybe. I turned on all the lights, opened the door, and stepped outside. I was naked.

"Robert Klassen?" the head man said. Black. Black uniforms, black belts, black boots, black helmets, black assault rifles. All black. "State your name, mister."

"Robert Klassen."

"Hold it right there, mister." I hadn't moved. Two men went past me into the trailer. I listened to them trashing the place. "Why are you naked?" the head man said.

"I didn't have time to dress," I said. He looked puzzled. "Throw some clothes out here," he commanded.

Shirt, jeans, and sandals landed on the ground and I put them on.

"Okay, mister, let's get in the van." He waved his assault rifle off to the left. I started to move, then he said, "Wait." He came up behind me and grabbed my right arm. I screamed and fell. "What the fuck?" he yelled.

"Arthritis," I cried.

I don't remember the next few minutes, I was in too much pain. I was shackled, arms and legs, chained to a ring in the floor. Four men in black, visors down, guarded me. The van sped away.

I spent the first night in a padded cell, a sixty-watt bulb in its wire cage ten-feet above illuminating nothing. It stunk of urine and shit. I pissed in a corner. I meditated, reached a certain state, then slept for a while.

"State your name." The man in military uniform was blond and about the age of my youngest son. He had blue eyes, too, but his were killer's eyes, the eyes of a psychopath, cold and devoid of feeling.

"Robert Klassen."

"Your age and occupation."

"Sixty-two and retired."

The man stared at me. "You're a writer," he said.

"Yes, I write."

"That's an occupation."

"No. It's a hobby. I don't make any money."

The man wrote something on the form. The room was small, about ten by twelve, and painted olive green. There were no windows, only a table and two chairs, a steel door, and a caged light bulb overhead. It stunk of sweat and something else, I couldn't figure out what.

"Okay," the man said, looking up, "now tell me about your family."

"Parents dead, wives divorced, three kids, alienated, no girl friends, no pets. That's it."

The man looked at his form. "You have a brother."

"Oh, yeah. I always forget him. We're not close."

"Who are your friends?"

"Hmmmm. Haven't got any I know about."

"Not likely," the man said, consulting his form again. "Who is this Sarah?"

"Former landlady. I rented a room from her."

"You didn't sleep with her?"

"Not as I recall."

The man made another note. He stared at me again. "You're lying."

"If you say so."

I spent that night in a cell with a toilet. The bed was bolted to the floor and to the wall. Somebody slipped a food tray through a slot in the steel door. I flushed the food. Then I meditated.

People want to live and to thrive. They count on that. But what is the proper attitude for a prisoner of the state? To want to live and thrive? I have committed no crime against mankind, until they made it a crime to speak one's mind. You are the criminals, I told them, you are killing social order, you are killing society, you are killing civilization, and they imprison me for saying so. Should I respond by wanting to live and thrive? I don't think so.

This man wore a suit and tie and looked for all the world like an aspiring attorney. "Mr. Klassen," he said, sprightly, "why haven't you objected to your arrest?"

"I didn't know I was arrested."

"But the police came in the night and took you away. Isn't that arrest?"

"I'd call it abduction."

"And you don't protest?"

"I am not armed. They were armed. You are armed."

"Ah, but you would protest if you were armed!"

"Who knows? The fact is, I was not and I am not armed."

"But you might have, right?"

"I doubt it. I can't fire a gun."

"And why can't you fire a gun, Mr. Klassen? Do you have a thing about guns?"

"No. I have arthritis."

"I see." The man looked confused. He dug into his briefcase and pulled out a file. "I have some questions here about your friends."

"Good. I'd like to know who they are."

Now he was annoyed. "I have here your email correspondence going back for six months."

"Okay."

"Why don't you use PGP?"

"I have nothing to hide."

"I don't believe that's true. You write in code. I want to know that code."

"I don't write in code."

"You wrote: 'That explains the shark attacks. They're not sharks! They're really Arab terrorist scuba divers! Now I have two questions. What do they do with their turbans? And how can you learn to scuba dive in sand?' What does this mean, Mr. Klassen?"

I laughed until I cried. "Sorry, Mr. Spook," I said at last, "it means that you are a fool."

They left me in solitary for seven days and for seven days I flushed the food. Without medications my heart was fluttering and missing and pounding in bewildering cycles, though I hardly paid attention. My mind was trapped in withdrawal. Cold turkey.

"What kind of a world do you think we live in?"

This was a faux-blond lady dressed in a tweed suit. No make-up. Severe. Anal-retentive.

"You are a killer," I said, "I am a thinker. In what kind of world does a killer interrogate a thinker?"

"Answer my question."

"You just did."

After that session they put me into a cell with six Arabic speaking boys in their twenties. Late at night one of the boys came to my cot and leaned over me.

"Sick?" he said.

I nodded.

"Die?" he said.

I nodded.

He took my hand and he knelt down and he prayed.

ICELAND: A LIBERTARIAN MODEL?

2002

Correspondents have suggested that the original organization of Iceland society represents a model for libertarian limited government, somewhat analogous to the original organization of our Thirteen Colonies. To learn more about this issue I consulted:

ORDERED ANARCHY, STATE, AND RENT-SEEKING:
THE ICELANDIC COMMONWEALTH, 930-1262
by Birgir T. Runolfsson Solvason

http://www.hi.is/~bthru/ritgerd.html

This 1991 dissertation is about Iceland between the 10th and 13th century, the so-called Commonwealth period. Iceland was populated by people escaping the political chaos in Denmark, Norway, and maybe England and Ireland. They were mostly Viking families. As they settled the uninhabited land, they formed local and then regional governing committees to settle disputes and to judge criminals. They had no ruling elite at first, but committee members were all were property owners. Crimes were paid by restitution and punished by banishment, either temporary or permanent.

The people who colonized this hostile environment did so to escape from their Kings' wars. Although illiterate, they were wise enough to avoid creating another monarchy. They believed in private property and in reciprocal cooperation, but they brought with them the nagging social problems that affect all human societies, dependent individuals. At first, orphaned children, isolated sick people, and lone infirm old people were parceled out to healthy families by the local committee depending on the burden those families could handle. In bad years of need, the sick, the young, and the old were left outdoors to freeze. So when the local chiefs offered a welfare service to care for these people through the church in exchange for an annual tithe of 1% on all personal property, the people accepted the idea.

The problem these primitive people could neither foresee nor forestall resided in that authority to tax. That power was given to those local individuals who were also their leading farmers, judges, and priests. An individual's temptation to expand his power to collect this easy money became irresistible and territorial civil war was inevitable. By 1264 the war-weary people of Iceland had given themselves to the protection of the King of Norway. Individualism built this society and socialism destroyed it.

The American people have made exactly the same mistakes. Listening to the same siren songs from political government, and despite our brief introduction to the innovation of private insurance, we have accepted the idea of paying taxes for welfare and warfare.

Is it too late to turn back? The people of Iceland made their seminal mistake by adopting domestic taxation within six-generations of their settlement and it took one and a half centuries of civil war to result in the end of their independence from a centralized state. One could argue that the people of America similarly made their seminal mistake by adopting domestic taxation within six generations of their settlement and that we also lost our independence from the centralized state in roughly one and a half centuries (WWII). Although there are distinct differences in the manner in which domestic taxation affected each society, the results are remarkably similar. Once a people have traded their sense of self-reliance for a sense of co-dependency wrought through taxation, their society has nearly sealed its fate.

Do we now search for an equivalent of a King of Norway to come forth and save us from our folly? How about a One-World Political State? This dream of centuries of scheming warlords has not gone away. The United Nations wants to tax the world (read U.S.) for the welfare of mankind. The siren sings. Some people even listen. Is it an accident that this proposal is made public as the American Imperial War Machine rolls across the planet? War and Welfare Forever! Or to complete the Marxist rationalization of Lord Keynes, "In the long run we're all dead" at the same time.

Solvason concludes:

> The forced cooperation through the Hreppar [committee], within an otherwise voluntary associated structure, and residency requirement also make it harder for anyone to claim that the Commonwealth was in any significant way an example of libertarianism in practice.

The Commonwealth was a limited political government, but a political government nonetheless, and as such it failed to provide the security and justice that it promised. Political government always fails. If human society is to endure beyond our "time of troubles," as Toynbee called such times as we live in today, the one concept or organizing principle we must supersede is political government.

The alternative, as Hans-Herman Hoppe concluded in his book, *Democracy, The God That Failed*, is to "…finally allow insurance agencies to do what they are destined to do…" (pg.292)—that is, to replace the promises of political government with private contracts for security and justice—with a money-back guarantee for success.

Previously published at http://www.lewrockwell.com

THE GOLDEN RULE

2002

Do unto others as you would have others do unto you. How many ways can we say the same thing backwards?

If you want other people to hate you, then hate other people.

If you want other people to attack you, then attack other people.

If you want other people to steal, then steal from other people.

If you want other people to murder, then murder other people.

If you want your civilization destroyed, then destroy another civilization.

The most elementary observation of human social behavior reveals a pattern called reciprocal response, otherwise known as tit for tat. This observation was first independently described around two-thousand, six-hundred years ago in India by the Buddha, in China by Confucius, and in Greece by Socrates, although I imagine that the observation did not go unnoticed by people in prehistoric times.

One characteristic of the reciprocal response in the history of societies and of civilizations is the cumulative effect of reinforcement on either positive behavior or negative behavior. As the negative behavior of one society escalates with respect to a neighboring society, so the negative behavior of the neighbor escalates in response; we saw this clearly during the Cold War and we are seeing again today in the Middle East. As the positive behavior of one society escalates with respect to a neighboring society, so the positive behavior of the neighbor escalates in response; we saw this beginning to happen during the industrialization of America and the growth of world trade between the political tyranny of Lincoln and the political tyranny of Wilson, a fleeting window of opportunity that may come to be viewed as America's Golden Age—if there are any human beings left to view it.

The Golden Rule operates in human society whether we like it or not. It is not a moral principle and it is not a law of nature, but it is the way humans interact. I have lived in communities all over North America and everywhere the overwhelming majority of people are friendly, helpful, industrious, and private, just like me. Now I communicate with individuals all over the planet and I get the same response. But if we are all such nice people, why do we all worry about nuclear winter and the end of mankind?

Because not all people are friendly, helpful, industrious, and private, and those few people are the ones who rule the rest of us through political government. They are the defectors from the Golden Rule, criminals, and they believe, in psychopathic hubris, that they can beat the Rule. The warlords whom Confucius advised to treat the people justly ignored him and thus vindicated his warning—or else you will perish. The warlords today are well advised to heed the Rule, because even they will perish in consequence of denying it. I wonder if they really care about that?

Previously published at http://www.lewrockwell.com

ACCELERATING DISASTER

2002

Fred Reed recently posted an article entitled *Going Faster and Faster: The Acceleration of Decline* http://www.fredoneverything.net/Declne.html on the decay of morality in America since 1964. I can't argue with him. Many, many people of our generation have noticed it and complained about it. There doesn't seem to be anything we can do to stop it. Fred Reed lays the blame on our educational system and on our media. I believe he is correct, but I also believe the root cause goes much deeper in our society.

Science tells us that contradictions can't exist, that is, that one thing cannot be its opposite at the same time. Thus, according to the law of gravity, you can't fall up. In human social matters, however, contradictions abound. Thus, while a political government tells society they are there to protect us, the same political government turns around and destroys the society that supports it. That's 100% historical reality. It appears that practicing hypocrites will run into inescapable problems with reality sooner or later. I think our society is colliding with its own contradictions right now.

Like it or not, American culture was rooted in Greco-Roman traditions, in Christianity, and in English Common Law. These roots never were entirely compatible with each other. Without thinking too precisely about who owns what, our political founders wrote these contradictions into our

Constitution, which immediately resulted in the Whiskey Rebellion, a tax revolt. Article One, Section Nine protected slavery, one Greco-Roman tradition that contradicts Christianity and one that required hypocrites to defend it in Common Law.

Further contradictions would be exploited as politicians discovered them. So within two generations Lincoln launched the savage war that violated all American cultural heritage. The survivors of that terror had children and their grandchildren went to die in the trenches of France. Survivors of that terror had children who went to die all over the planet. Survivors of that terror had children who grew up with the daily threat of nuclear holocaust and who finally went to die in Southeast Asia. The survivors of that terror had children who can't read, don't care, ingest drugs, kill each other, and generally act like uncivilized savages who have no cultural heritage at all. They're right. They don't. Our children have inherited the consequences of two-centuries of contradictions, including slavery, Sherman's civilian extermination, Mustard gas, Dresden, Hiroshima, the Cold War, and, finally, Imperial War, all nicely documented in bleeding color on television, on the Internet, and in news media everywhere. What will come of this?

I don't know. I live by *The Golden Rule* and I taught my children to live by it as well. I believe that people in any society live by the golden rule, whether they know it or not, in the selfish desire to keep on living and thriving. That purpose itself may not exist inside the corrupt society inside the most corrupt and dangerous Capital on Earth, the society that Fred Reed describes, but I see that purpose still pursued elsewhere. Political governments are bringing about the collision of contradictions against this reality: people want to live and thrive. Political coercion is not compatible with this purpose; political coercion is not compatible with the golden rule; so we've got this problem.

Two centuries of political contradictions have effectively severed our culture from its roots, but no political government can sever the connection between the human desire to live and thrive and the natural way to accomplish it, following the golden rule. What political government can do and has done throughout history, in order to defend its own accumulation of contradictions, is to destroy its own society. Our current political regime is doing exactly that.

What can we do about it? Nothing much that I can see; hope we survive, pray we survive, study alternatives, teach the children who want to learn, and damn the people who brought us to this pass.

Previously published at http://www.lewrockwell.com

OLD NEWS

2001

Let's call it a ninety-day bloodless coup d'etat. Well, nearly bloodless. Close enough to bloodless. All power to the executive! Isn't this something Presidents dream? Or maybe not just Presidents. What do wannabe Presidents dream? Does the common person dream of such power? I doubt it. The common person has better things to dream about, like the job, the mortgage, the food on the table, and the kids' education. So the common person dreams about common things and the President dreams about power over the common person. That is old news, very old news.

I wonder, as a common person, why we permit the executive to rule us willy-nilly and why we pay for it? They have given us a lot of excuses to permit them the power over the years. Once there were the Nazi Party and the Communist Party threats for us to fight with our own lives and our own money, but those threats petered out. Then there was Poverty to Fight and, Good Lord, Drugs! Certainly the parents who grew up smoking dope cannot tolerate their children growing up smoking dope! Certainly not! And the executive must prosecute these wars against something or other because the common person lacks the will or the power or the brains to do it personally. We all know that. That these executive wars have been total failures is not to be mentioned in public. It's a state secret.

I won't mention the Iran-Contra scandal, I doubt if anybody remembers it anyway, but the fact remains that the turf wars over drugs, guns, and oil are still on the executive agenda and we, the common people, are still paying to wage these wars. Now that the executive has assumed all power, we the common people, can expect to be snuffed out for complaining about their wars and about the extortion enacted against us. The executive tells us, shut up, or we will shut you up.

A similar thing happened in Athens long ago. A similar thing happened in Rome a few centuries later. Now it's happening to us. It's old news.

Previously published at http://www.lewrockwell.com

WARMONGERS

2001

Warmongers puzzle me. A warmonger is: "One who advocates or attempts to stir up war." What motivates these people?

I suppose that in some primitive hunter-gatherer societies, a warmonger could be seeking to expand food producing territory or to gain ritual tribal status or to enact revenge on a neighboring society; Homer describes these motives well, although his societies were of a higher order of sophistication than, say, the archaic Inuit Eskimos, about whom we don't hear of such behavior. One might say that warmongering arises where one society has something that another society wants to steal by force, as the Hyksos wanted to steal the wealth of Egypt, although there is the personal component of acquiring raw power over the lives of people that may attract some individuals to war. Greed and power, then, are most likely the prime motives of the warmonger in historical times.

But what about today? Why would already rich and powerful Americans want to put both their money and their prestige at risk to promote war? Sure, the state can extort a million dollars from the taxpayers and use it to build a Patriot missile for the express purpose of blowing it up and destroying somebody else's life and property and I suppose that some part of that million goes into a warmonger's pocket. Is war, then, simply another way to transfer wealth from the taxpayer to the rich by force and fraud?

I should stop here and ask, how did the rich warmongers get rich in the first place? Unfortunately, I don't know. It's reported that the revolving door between the public sector and the private sector pumps millions of tax dollars into well-known pockets, proving that people who make the laws know how to evade them. But what about the wealthy warmongers who don't have their fingers in the public till? Did they get rich by force and fraud as well?

I wonder. When a man puts up a half-a-million dollars to fund an organization explicitly created to criminalize American freedom of speech, I wonder what's in it for him? To sell the idea of another world war to a disillusioned American people requires silencing opposition in general and Lew Rockwell in particular, that much is obvious, but where is the real return to this man's investment? Does he merely want to direct the firing squad or run the gulag for American dissident writers?

That doesn't make sense to me. What does make sense is a far larger ambition, like the ambition of Alexander, Julius Caesar, Napoleon, Hitler, Stalin, and Mao, to enslave the whole of mankind under one ruler in a One World State. Would the wealthy warmonger desire that kind of power for himself? Or would he prefer to be the power behind the power? Not the King, but the King-Maker?

I wish I knew the answer. Warmongers puzzle me.

Previously published at http://www.lewrockwell.com

WARMONGERS II

2002

In my first exploration of this subject, I could not figure out what motivates the warmongers in America. I thought about the usual suspects, money and power, and the revolving door in the District of Criminals, where today's politician is tomorrow's CEO, but I rejected them as rational explanations. That was my mistake. The warmongers don't live in a rational world.

Once upon a time I subscribed to a neocon newsletter because I was curious about their supporting arguments. I discovered that it was pretty much nonsense written by aging armchair warriors missing the old testosterone, so I dropped my subscription. Imagine my surprise when one of these newsletters arrived in my mailbox today! It consisted of several long rants against the evil Saddam and it demanded that America initiate a war against Iraq. Nary a rational argument existed.

Let's think about this. America's allies in Western Civilization are opposed to attacking Iraq again, excepting Toady Blair, of course. America's allies in the Middle-East are opposed to attacking Iraq. America's trading partners in the Far East are sitting calmly with folded hands and smiling at a joke they're not sharing with us. So what are we doing? Is America on the verge of making a Very Bad Mistake?

Just for fun I looked up the median age of Middle-Eastern populations http://www.prcdc.org/summaries/middleeast/middleeast.html and found that it consists largely of fighting-age young folks with plenty of testosterone. By comparison with American fighting-age young folks, the prognosis for an all out war in the region doesn't look good, even with smart bombs, although the warmongers are calling for nuclear bombs instead, and that might work.

But then the question arises, who is going to fight in this war? True, the Baby Boomer generation has been remarkably silent about the warmongers' activities over the past decade, and some pollsters claim they will continue to shut up and pay, but this time it's *their* kids who will be drafted for cannon fodder, *their* kids who are just graduating from college and starting families and new careers, *their* kids who will die at the hands of the warmongers. Are they going to stand for that?

Maybe. It's too much to ask of this generation that they connect the dots between the Federal Reserve, the stock market crash, the Pentagon and its contractors, the Patriot Act, the November elections, and the suddenly urgent need to start World War Three in the Middle-East, but when the body bags start coming home, they might get the message.

The time to stop the warmongers is NOW.

Previously published at http://www.lewrockwell.com

THE DRAFT

2002

Response to my last column was instructive. Some readers believed that my reference to the draft was cynical and unjustified. Perhaps many Americans cannot believe that Congress would inflict this unconstitutional enslavement on American youth once again, especially those whose memory of the violent protests against it thirty-years ago are still fresh. For those readers I have some bad news.

House Resolution 3598 was introduced in Congress last December; it is called the "Universal Military Training and Service Act of 2001." (The best way to find the text is to go to http://www.rcnv.org/rcnv/co.htm and follow instructions.) Like whatever the Patriot Act was called as it gathered dust waiting for the right moment, this resolution likewise waits. And as you read this document do keep in mind the assurances that the Patriot Act only applied to foreigners, a blatant lie, as we know now, and remember the new powers usurped to use US military forces to police civilians inside the United States. Here is the heart of the matter:

SEC. 3. BASIC MILITARY TRAINING AND EDUCATION.

(a) OBLIGATION FOR YOUNG MEN—It is the obligation of every male citizen of the United States, and every other male person residing in the United States, who is between the ages of

18 and 22 to receive basic military training and education as a member of the armed forces unless the citizen or person is exempted under the provisions of this Act.

(b) ACCEPTANCE OF YOUNG WOMEN VOLUNTEERS— Female citizens of the United States, and other female persons residing in the United States, who are between the ages of 18 and 22 may volunteer for enlistment in the armed forces to receive basic military training and education under this Act. At the discretion of the Secretary concerned, the Secretary concerned may accept such volunteers to receive such training and education.

Upon graduation from high school, young men no longer need to worry about their next step in life, because they are going to boot camp. Willing young women can go with them. If they didn't learn to obey orders in school, they will learn to obey orders now. And lest any high school dropouts think they're home free:

(b) EXTENDED TRAINING AND EDUCATIONAL SER-VICES FOR HIGH SCHOOL DROPOUTS—A person inducted as a conscript or accepted as a volunteer pursuant to this Act who has not obtained a high school diploma or its equivalent, shall receive basic military training and education as a member of one of the armed forces for an additional period of up to six months after the completion of the period established for members of that armed force under subsection (a). The Secretary concerned shall assist such members in earning the equivalent of a high school diploma while receiving their basic military training and education.

Isn't that thoughtful of them! The jackboot standing guard outside your home might even be able to read his orders.

The only man in Congress who stood up against this draconian legislation was Dr. Ron Paul http://www.counterpunch.org/pauldraft.html.

The District of Criminals have all of their pieces in place. They have eliminated the Bill Of Rights. They have eliminated the Posse Comitatus Act. The Executive has usurped the authority to rule alone http://membrane.com/pac/crises/War.html. Now all they need is the manpower to enforce that rule. And it's waiting there.

The time to stop the warmongers is NOW.

Previously published at http://www.lewrockwell.com

TERRORISM?

2001

On September 3, 2001, the FBI shot and killed Mr. Tom Crosslin at his private campground outside Vandelia, Michigan. On September 4, 2001, the FBI shot and killed and possibly castrated Mr. Rolland Rohm at the same location <http://www.heraldpalladium.com/archives/index.inn? loc=detail&doc=/2001/October/31-707-news5 >. Despite all of the misery following the 9/11 attack on America, I hope that the murders of these two Americans will not be forgotten. Vandelia deserves to be remembered alongside Ruby Ridge and Waco.

Crosslin, 47, stood for something the local authorities did not approve. He endorsed the legalization of marijuana. Moreover, he used his Rainbow Farm campground as a gathering place for like-minded people. Although there appears to be no substantial evidence that marijuana was consumed during these gatherings, he was arrested. The court told him, no more gatherings on your property. He held another gathering. The court issued a summons for him to appear. He didn't show up. The cops came to arrest him and he, holding a hunting rifle, told them to get off his property. Sound familiar?

I happened to be in southern Michigan on August 31 and I spotted the headline about the armed standoff in a local newspaper. I speculated on the question of how long it would take for the FBI killers to show up. I was wrong by a week. They not only showed up promptly, they completed their dirty business almost overnight. The outrage amongst supporters of Mr. Crosslin's cause had already sped around the planet on the Internet and plans were underway to import supporters to the site. Before any of this could happen, the FBI killed the man. End of protest.

The murder of Mr. Rohm is puzzling. After all, their principal target was already dead. The press reports imply that the two men were homosexuals, with dark undertones about their relationship to Mr. Crosslin's thirteen-year old son. This would make Mr. Rohm's murder a gratuitous hate-crime in any other set of circumstances not involving the FBI. They say he was also holding a hunting rifle and so they shot him. Sure. And maybe he castrated himself.

Today we are assured that the FBI is there to protect us from terrorists. I wonder about that. True, the FBI has some convincing assassins working for the department, at least against American citizens. Now that the Bill of Rights is in the toilet again, they can arrest and interrogate each and every one of us if they feel like it. They can torture us for fun or kill us with malice and still go home to the wife and kids with a clear conscience, if they had one, because they are protected by the law.

What the hell is terrorism anyway? Wherein is the FBI unlike the KGB or the Gestapo? When the local cops give them a call, don't they just drop in and murder the malcontents? I'll tell you what, I'm scared. I'm not scared of anthrax, or even smallpox, and I'm not scared of Muslims, I'm scared of the psychopathic personality disorders employed by the state to police ordinary citizens like myself. I'm scared of our government and its FBI. Is that not terrorism?

What To Do?

2002

Wally Conger recently reminded us to remember the FBI murders at Ruby Ridge http://www.lewrockwell.com/orig3/conger3.html on its tenth anniversary, August 21. Less well known, we can also remember the first anniversary of the FBI murders at Vandelia, Michigan, where they shot and killed Tom Crosslin at his private campground http://www.heraldpalladium.com/archives/index.inn?loc=detail&doc=/2001/October/31 -707-news5 (Keyword: Crosslin) on September 3 and his friend Rolland Rohm on September 4. Both events were similar in set-up, stand-off, and sniping, except in speed of execution; evidently the FBI had learned that time was of the essence, and there was no messy media event at Vandelia. These murders, as well as the ones at Waco and Wounded Knee, make me doubt the wisdom of private citizens staging an armed confrontation with the professional killers employed by the State.

People should own guns for self-defense. The Second Amendment was clearly aimed at private defense against tyrannical government, but in those days it was most likely to be muskets versus muskets, not deer rifles versus assault weapons and precision sniper rifles, not to mention tanks. Nor was it likely that a state militia in those days was any better trained in killing than the average settler, they were one and the same, while today the trained killer has spent hundreds of paid hours practicing his trade. To put it bluntly, those who believe that Americans could successfully rise up in arms against tyranny are dreaming.

Since WWII there have been innumerable civilian revolts against governments around the world, but the spontaneous eruption of people with arms against armored troop carriers and tanks and Apache helicopters has only been useful for clips and bites on the evening news, while the people have been slaughtered, and their property destroyed. Moreover, our government has been planning for this contingency since the violent anti-war protests thirty years ago, and they have held military training in the streets of our cities. There is more than ample evidence to prove that this is not the way to go.

I am a good listener. I hear what people are saying at work, at the supermarket, in the malls, and what I hear is suspicion of State propaganda and anger at the outright lies fed to us by the media. Americans are not ignorant, they're just busy, but once the word about THE DRAFT escapes from the dustbins of newspaper editors and television producers, I believe that Americans will find the time to speak loud enough for all to hear. (And did not whispers of the draft stop the Bush I and the Clinton thrust for power?) Nobody likes a trap, and the trap is set. Speak up, and speak out.

The political-military-industrial complex relies as heavily on information technology as business and industry in general, and nearly all of us as individuals. Once again, I urge IT professionals to think about what they are doing. Is your work promoting liberty, or is your work promoting slavery? For this is the history of political government repeating itself, and we can easily look to the past to foresee the future. Upon your decision the fate of mankind may hang in the balance.

Whereas I would like to ignore the State altogether and get on with my own business, I admit that since 9/11 my cause has shifted somewhat to stop our political government's plunge into tyranny, but that is not a call to arms. American college students are not going to like being drafted again, and I encourage them to resist and to protest. I likewise encourage their parents to resist and to protest American Imperialism, and to regain our Bill Of Rights. Repeal the Patriot Act. Repeal ALL Executive Orders, and forbid that tyrannical practice. Given that much, while we would still be saddled with massive government theft and interference with our lives, we could still have some confidence in our continuing existence, and not the growing uncertainty about our future.

The time to stop the tyranny is NOW.

Previously published at http://www.lewrockwell.com

AMERICAN DAD

2002

I grew up on a small Indiana farm during the 1940s and 1950s. Dad was a farmer and a businessman, a civic leader, and a parish advisor. He was a quiet, sober, industrious man, who was also generous and friendly, with a great sense of humor. He had little education, but he was well read; he could recite poetry and Shakespeare and recount the histories of American innovators and entrepreneurs, whom he greatly admired. He cared little or nothing for politics, although he occasionally voiced contempt for the state and its wars.

I absorbed many of my dad's attitudes while I was growing up. Thus I felt protective of our property and resentful of state imposed quotas on farm products, wartime rationing, the military draft, and taxation. At an early age, I felt that these state intrusions on our private lives were unjust, a sentiment that was common in our community at the time. But times were changing.

I didn't know it, but many of the teachers in our community high school were hard-core socialists who did the best they could to shape our opinions of socialist political programs. Thus when I wrote a paper on the marvels of Swedish socialism for my sophomore English class, my dad hit the roof. Then he explained the difference between private charity and socialist redistribution of wealth, and the difference between controlling your own life and having it controlled by the state. I got the message, but I'm afraid that many of my classmates did not.

Dad didn't care much for Joe McCarthy either. While he clearly disapproved of socialist propaganda in the high school, he regarded the House Un-American Activities Committee as an anti-Constitutional police-state tribunal whose sole purpose was acquisition of power, not justice. Watching the Enron witch-hunts today reminds me of dad's comments on the newsreels we watched during the fifties.

I was raising a family in northern California when Vietnam triggered widespread civil disobedience in America. While I supported the effort, I also worried that it would provoke martial law, something like the Patriot Act and the Presidential Star Chamber we've got today, that would endanger the future of my children. Dad told me, don't worry too much about it, the world has been going to hell all my life and we haven't arrived there yet. Somehow I did not feel reassured.

I don't recall preaching to my children, though I did not hesitate to correct the misinformation they were taught in school. I guess I was following in my father's footsteps, as they say. I wanted them to recognize social problems and to solve them on their own, if they could, or discuss them, if they couldn't. That approach worked and we continue to discuss the finer details of problem-solving today. As independent adults, they don't like people telling them what to think or what to do and they don't like having the results of their endeavors stolen from them year after year.

Now I ask you, was my dad anti-American? Am I anti-American? Are my children anti-American? My family firmly believes in the absolute ownership and control of our private property, including our lives, wealth, and innovations. Our family firmly condemns slavery, including tax slavery, chattel slavery, and conscription slavery. Our family firmly supports freedom of speech, freedom of religion, and freedom of action. Our family accepts Constitutional government even knowing that it is coercive government. Our family rejects tyranny. Is that anti-American? AVOT says it is http://64.224.126.170/stories/storyReader$26.

Americans For Victory Over Terrorism believes that we are sheeple to be herded according to their will. They seek to redefine an American as a slave. They seek to silence true Americans. They are the anti-American voice.

Dad would say, beware, we're almost there.

Previously published at http://www.lewrockwell.com

WHAT DO YOU KNOW?

2002

Dad used to ask me, "What do you know for sure today?" He was not given to joking around, but he always asked that question with a little smile, like it was some kind of secret joke. He didn't ask the question very often, either, so it always came as a little surprise. At the age of ten, I just hemmed and hawed, and I felt uncomfortable; I didn't know the answer. As a teen-ager, I believe that I resented the question because I had begun to think about it, and I still couldn't answer it.

It's a good question, and a good trick to make a kid think, although I would phrase it differently for an adult. How do you know for sure that what you think you know is true? I have learned that this is not an easy question to answer; I have read maybe a hundred pounds of books out of the ton of literature on this question, and I've only come to a handful of "for sure" answers.

Scientists have developed a method for coping with the issue of truth in knowledge. First, somebody observes something in nature that calls for an explanation, like why is the ocean horizon on a clear day curved, not straight? Second, some guesses, hypotheses, are dreamed up, like maybe the Earth is round, maybe the Earth is a flat disk, or maybe somebody's vision is defective. Third, some kind of test of the hypothesis is devised, like send a ship out there to see if it falls off the edge, or if it comes back

51

with relevant information. Fourth, make more observations of the likely facts to verify the hypothesis, like sail out of sight of land to see if the horizon is curved all around. Fifth, make a simple statement of the truth so that anybody, anywhere, anytime, can verify it, like the Earth is a sphere. That would be knowledge, for sure.

That would also be pretty simple science, for as we learn more, the more we have to learn. One of the big arguments in science began in the Seventeenth Century: is light a wave, or a particle? http://www.nsf.gov/nstw_questions/phys/quest063.htm Folks devised tests to prove it either way, so the argument raged until a bright young man http://www.aip.org/history/heisenberg/ in the Twentieth Century said that light is both, depending on how you test it. This didn't go down well with the "what my net can't catch isn't fish" crowd http://www-gap.dcs.st-and.ac.uk/~history/Quotations/Eddington.html, and the scientific method itself was called into question, as we have seen in the global warming controversy http://www.gfdl.gov/~gth/web_page/article/aree_page6.html. How ever the Uncertainty Principle may have undermined confidence in the scientific method in the "softer" sciences, it has enabled physicists to make new discoveries about the nature of the universe we live in, and observational facts still count.

Early success in physics led to the emergence of chemistry from its ancient cocoon of alchemy by using the scientific method. Imitation in biology, and the applied technology of medicine, led to mixed results; Pasteur's hypothesis tested true, while Darwin's hypothesis tested plausible, yet remains doubtful. Meanwhile, medicine rests on solid science in some areas, like bacteriology, while it embraces popular fads in treatment based on statistical results of trial and error studies that are too often biased, and even fraudulent. Hypotheses in the subjects of psychology and sociology cannot be tested, so these are not sciences, but only the selective subjective speculations of some individuals about the nature of mankind. Then we arrive at political science, a dreadful oxymoron, and a fraud.

I believe that the scientific method is a valid intellectual tool for discovering the truth as long as the knowledge we're searching for is not charged with political intent, that is, somebody's desire to use it to justify their coercion against other people. Politicians don't use the scientific method, politicians appeal to sentiment to get their way, and they seldom resort to factual evidence to support their arguments. This tactic has been adopted by many special-interest groups as well, both among the elite and the common people; pseudo-science is so politically correct that it is not to be questioned, and students who are drilled in it have no way to discover the truth unless they defect from the group, and think for themselves.

So a President can lead us into global warfare on the basis of no evidence whatever, and get away with it, because people believe what he says is true. But what he says is not true, and there is abundant evidence for that http://www.moveon.org/moveonbulletin/bulletin4.html. He's making it up, he's fabricating evidence, he's lying, as they have all been lying to us for decades. Maybe we're so used to fabrications that we've forgotten how to look for the truth. "The size of the lie is a definite factor in causing it to be believed," said Adolph Hitler http://centre.telemanage.ca/quotes.nsf/quotes/839a515594de8a9385256969005d3417. His successors in political crime have learned this lesson well; they are telling us some whoppers these days.

What do you know for sure today?

Thanks, Dad.

Previously published at http://www.lewrockwell.com

Opportunity Knocking

2002

One June 16, 2002, CNN.com reported,
http://www.cnn.com/2002/ALLPOLITICS/06/15/sc.plutonium/index.h
tml "The federal Energy Department is scheduled to ship the plutonium
from the Rocky Flats weapons plant in Colorado—which is being
closed—to South Carolina's Savannah River nuclear weapons complex,
where it will be used as fuel for a nuclear power plant." South Carolina
governor Jim Hodges declared a state of emergency. He intends to have
the state police stop the TRUCKS.

Think about that for a minute.

Let's pretend this is fiction. Let's say that you own some plutonium in
Colorado that you sell to me in South Carolina. How would we arrange to
ship it? By road, by rail, or by air?

We could truck it over a couple of thousand miles of taxway, I mean free-
way, that passes through a dozen major metropolitan cities, but we decide
that would be pretty stupid. Even with a military convoy to protect the
trucks, some crazy driving a little compact car loaded with explosives
could nail one of the trucks in one of myriad bottle-necks that riddle the
taxway system in cities.

We could ship it by rail, but that not only poses the same hazard, it introduces the new hazard of train wreck on our old and poorly maintained rail system.

Finally, we decide to ship it by air and we call UPS. Now that sounds risky too, and it is, but people have been flying nuclear bombs around the planet for decades without a mishap, so it can't be that risky. We would also decide to keep this shipment secret, very secret.

In fact, of course, all of the decisions in this matter are made by federal bureaucrats who have no personal or proprietary stake in it. They decided to ship it by truck. And far from being secret, the shipment has been advertised all over the world, probably even in Arabic.

One governor is standing up for the safety of the people in his state. Or maybe he is grandstanding, it doesn't matter. What are the other governors saying? Is this shipment going through Kansas City? Chicago? Washington? Is anybody else worried about this dirty bomb rolling through town?

This project is so stupid it makes me wonder about the sanity of the people involved.

I wonder if anybody told the FBI yet?

Previously published at http://www.lewrockwell.com

A New National Holiday

2001

December 11, 2001, America was celebrated in political capitals around the world. I saw it on television news. While I did not doubt the origin of this celebration and its careful timing, I did wonder what exactly was being celebrated? The World War on Terrorism? The defeat of the Taliban? The marvel of American military force? American Imperialism? Or driving home the final nail in the coffin of the American Revolution and of the Republic for which it stood. The Republic is dead and gone. American political government is now officially a tyranny.

> Tyranny is defined as: 1. A government in which a single ruler is vested with absolute power. 2. The office, authority, or jurisdiction of an absolute ruler. 3. Absolute power, especially when exercised unjustly or cruelly. 4.a. Use of absolute power. b. A tyrannical act. 5. Extreme harshness or severity; rigor.

Don't expect anybody to admit it anytime soon. Some Senators bristle at the term, although they delivered absolute power to the President without a qualm. One wonders why? But then the U.S. Congress has acted like a bunch of hapless schoolboys with their hands in the candy bowl for years; maybe their quid pro quo this time was the generous raise they gave themselves during this wartime recession, something else nobody is going to admit anytime soon.

So we, the viewing audience, are entertained by the spectacle of the Star Spangled Banner being played in Pakistan, recently an enemy, but now an ally, and everywhere else. The media claims that sixty nations are rallied around our flag and our anthem and our purpose and that the overwhelming majority of American taxpayers are likewise supporting World War Three, no matter what the cost in life, liberty, and property. This spectacle reminded me of something.

In 1959, William L. Shirer published his massive history called *The Rise And Fall Of The Third Reich*. Toward the end of Chapter Seven, he wrote:

(1934) "On August 19, some 95 per cent of those who had registered went to the polls, and 90 per cent, more than thirty-eight million of them, voted approval of Hitler's usurpation of complete power."

On September 4, a smiling Hitler appeared at the Nurnberg Reichsparteitag amidst the colorful waving flags and the patriotic anthems and thirty-thousand cheering Germans and he announced The Thousand Year Reich. Remember the film clips?

It makes me sad as we repeat the mistakes of our forefathers. I recall Mr. Shirer's warning: *"There will be no conquerors and no conquests, but only the charred bones of the dead on an uninhabited planet."* He was a wise man. Read his book.

Previously published at http://www.lewrockwell.com

JUSTICE

2001

The bumper sticker stuck to the refrigerator door behind the bar reads, "It ain't justice, it's just court." It's always the first thing I see when I walk in.

I generally go over to the bar every afternoon about four and order a pitcher of beer. The Lakeside Resort and Trailer Park was a hotspot during WWII. No more. The bar is a black hole in the daylight, smoky and stinking of human bodies and cigarettes and booze; light comes from the jukebox and the pool table and the television set that nobody ever turns off. The park itself isn't any better. The road is dusty and potholed and lined with tall weeds, water pipes leak, sewers stink, and wires dangle down from the maze overhead. The place is a dump. I like it because it is cheap and because I have a million-dollar view of the lake and the mountains from my old travel trailer and because the people who live there are, well, different—honest, you might say.

Depending on how hot the day has been, the rush hour into the parking lot begins about four. The pickup trucks roll in and big guys dressed in dirty jeans and sweaty tee-shirts and thick-soled boots stomp in and start yelling and drinking and shooting pool. The bartender turns up the jukebox and turns off the sound on the television. Wives and girlfriends show up from town and the park residents drift in one by one. Pretty soon they're three-deep at the bar and the place is packed. Everybody is smoking cigarettes.

Smoking in a bar would not have been a remarkable observation a few years ago and it still isn't in most places around the world, but in California today it's illegal. Who better understands how working people ought to live than Rob Reiner and his funny colleagues in Hollywood? Is it any mystery that this tiny minority has much in common with politicians? Or that they have uncommon clout in politics? Of course, they can afford the new fifty-cent per pack sin-tax on cigarettes and they can smoke and drink and snort what they like in their own bars, so what does it matter if they screw the underclass? I mean, if the working stiff is stupid enough to watch their movies, they're stupid enough to take orders from them too, right?

Wrong. The folks at the Lakeside Resort and Bar don't take kindly to being told what to do or what not to do, so the Hollywood master plan isn't working out too well there. The cops who like to prey on them individually on the streets in town are at least smart enough to leave them alone as a group in a bar. But what about that sin-tax? Would you believe that some folks will go through the trouble of buying their cigarettes out of state? You might even call some extremists smugglers. I noticed that some of these people would sometimes go to nearly any length to do what they were told not to do.

And vice versa. Common people can be stubborn. Several folks refuse to pay taxes. Maybe quite a few. It's not that they have some high moral purpose in refusing to pay taxes, they simply hate the system that collects the taxes. You see, most of these folks are ex-felons. Felony drunk driving, felony drug sales, felony this, felony that; no robbery or murder, mind you, nothing bad like that. One guy was taking a piss in his own front yard when a school bus drove past and he was arrested and convicted of public exposure and felony child abuse. Stuff like that. (Sure he was a jerk, but he wasn't a criminal.) So these people could not get a good, honest, payroll-tax kind of job if they wanted to because they are ex-felons, so each one has to find a way to make money under the table, which they do adroitly and quite admirably.

I was astonished by the many clever ways people contrive to make money, but I will not list them here for fear of exposing them to the enemy. Suffice it to say that the underground economy is alive and well in this country and that the good old American can-do spirit still thrives.

Okay, I suppose that some readers are thinking that this bar was a den of drugs and that the dirty, sweaty guys with thick-soled boots were all dealers, the sort of thing Hollywood likes to dream. Nope. These guys got dirty putting up sheet-rock or framing or plumbing or roofing or digging postholes or fixing engines. They are actually the buyers of certain drugs, like alcohol, nicotine, caffeine, and marijuana. There is a dealer living in the park, however, no surprise, under the remote supervision of the cops. The cops run the market for drugs in this town and woe to any enterprising interloper from the big city who tries to sell dope without a license.

I'm not making this up. Why would a rural resort and retirement community of thirteen-thousand residents need forty-two police cars, a fortified police station, a half-dozen cops on patrol day and night, and a barely literate police chief who owns twenty-two houses on a salary of a hundred-and-twenty thousand a year? Big-time money pours into and out of this city government and it doesn't come from little old ladies selling cookies. Residents joke about it. One resident, a tax-payer, by the way, and a good friend of mine, was shot by the cops for joking about it. So much for loud-mouthed Italian electricians; he won a substantial settlement from the city's insurance company in private arbitration for this crime. The cop went free.

One might think that a mild-mannered, middle-aged medical-technician and writer might feel threatened in such a rowdy low-life environment. Indeed, I will slink out the back door when the pool cues start flying, but I never feel like I am in danger of being robbed at home or mugged in the parking lot. I've lived in this town for twenty-years and I know almost everybody who lives in the park or who visits the bar. Some I have known as patients in the hospital. One of the first new friends I made was a gentleman who looks exactly like Santa Claus—except for the tattoos on his arms. He is, in fact, a retired machinist and a Hell's Angel. He is seventy-two and he likes my writing. Sometimes total strangers dressed in leathers and chains are buying me a beer at the bar. Somehow I feel safer here than I've felt in the San Francisco Hilton.

Some years ago, a physician with whom I worked in the emergency room, a man I truly respected, was accused of murdering a Native American child. Nine months after the alleged event, the cops and the feds arrested him in the emergency room and led him away in irons. Newspapers and wire services and television publicly convicted him then and there, just as the Grand Jury had done already in secret.

The legal ploy was transparent. First, a routine malpractice suit would have been settled out of court for peanuts, maybe a hundred-thousand, while millions were there for the taking after a murder conviction. Second, it was an election year and the State Attorney General needed a popular hit. Third, the feds wanted to destroy the secrecy of the medical peer review process mandated by the feds themselves.

The legal shift of focus from malpractice to murder had begun earlier in Denver, where nurses were charged with murder after a fatal medication error (the mistake was made by a pharmacist—who was not charged). It didn't take a genius to see that lawyers had discovered a new Mother Lode. Thousands of nuisance malpractice suits could be worth a fortune.

Needless to say, we in the medical business looked at it a little differently; if they can spin malpractice into murder, then we're all in the wrong business and it's time for us to get out.

Down at the Lakeside Resort and Trailer Park, the trial of our local doctor was a brisk topic in the bar. Many of the patrons knew him from past visits to the emergency room. I was prepared to defend him, but I didn't need to. These folks knew the score, they just weren't quite sure about the game. They were trying to figure out why the state had decided to persecute this man, they knew he wasn't guilty from the start.

After over a year of legal bickering in court, the now bankrupt doctor won over his tax-supported attackers and the case was dismissed, but not before the feds destroyed the privacy of medical peer review—any advice or censure doctors may offer their peers in these meetings is now a matter of public record in court. So they won't do it, of course. They'll hold their required meetings and they'll say nothing incriminating about anybody.

I drink my beer at the bar and I look at that bumper sticker on the refrigerator and I wonder where in hell do these lawyers think their world is going? The common, ordinary, working people of this country have no faith in the system and have no respect for the system; in fact, they hate the system. I sit and I wonder, why don't we change the system? Yes, indeed, why don't we?

I suppose you could interpret my point of view as a lawyer-bashing, a popular if futile gesture of rejection. I really don't feel that way, despite having been bashed myself by a couple of lawyers. I was favorably impressed by what happened to my gut-shot buddy in private and secret negotiations between lawyers representing different insurance companies in front of yet another lawyer representing neutral arbitration. I think he got a fair hearing and a decent settlement. I don't think that criminal prosecution of the cop who shot him would have accomplished a thing, aside from forcing the cop to search for honest work. We're not going to beat cops in court anyway, it's their system. Private arbitration is something different and more and more people are seeking it. It isn't perfect, but I think it's better than court. Sometimes it's almost like justice.

Previously published at http://www.lewrockwell.com

ABORTION

2001

I've never been pregnant. The mothers of my children always got pregnant, so I guess I'm about as qualified as any man to talk about abortion, a subject I'd rather not think about.

I don't approve of abortion in the sense that I would encourage a woman to get one, but I don't disapprove of abortion in the sense that I would endorse a state law that made it a crime for her to get one. I think that decision belongs to the woman. Here is why I think so.

My first observation is that a person owns her own life. Contrary to the implications of the possessive pronoun in our language, my wife is not my property. My wife belongs to herself. If you don't believe me, ask her. I claim the same for myself, that is, I own myself.

My second observation is that since a woman owns her own life, she must necessarily own her own body and her own mind. From that it follows that she owns the nutrients in her body and the ideas in her mind. The same goes for a man, too, of course.

A woman's life can produce derivatives, like children, money, new ideas, and waste products. Because a person owns her own life, a woman cannot own her children. Children own themselves. Here is where the issue of abortion always gets sticky.

The observational reality is that the life of the fetus is part of the life of the woman, and because the woman owns her own life, she owns the life of the fetus too. Therefore the decision to abort belongs to the woman.

However, the true nature of things means nothing if coercion is introduced. I mean, if the state decides to tell children that pi is equal to three, they can do it, although it isn't true.

Thus my first observation is immediately contradicted by the state. Nobody owns his or her life under the state. The state claims ownership of all life and all property within its jurisdiction and then allows pieces to dribble into controlled existence in exchange for tribute, commonly called taxes.

The state issues edicts by which we are ruled. Sometimes they make sense, sometimes they don't, but we know from experience that what may be legal today may become illegal tomorrow. Reality seems to become optional under the state. It isn't.

I still own my own life even if the state hangs me for saying it. A woman still owns her own life even if the state decrees that it's legal to abduct her and to buy her and sell her in a slave market. In the issue of abortion, the life of the fetus is the life of the woman; she alone owns it until it has a life of its own.

I would express gratitude to the pharmaceutical industry for offering a woman some control over her fertility. I would also express gratitude to the health-care industry for offering a woman a safe and painless abortion if she chooses. I would wish that the state would ignore the issue, but I know it won't.

Abortion is a hot political topic. A well advertised rally or debate will keep any number of people busy not paying attention to something else, like the mass murders we are committing in third-world countries. Instead, people raise the hue and cry about the morality of abortion.

Well, morality seems to expand and contract freely depending on circumstances. I figure that if a man lies, cheats, and steals, then he ought to pay for his crimes, but if he is judged by a pack of liars, cheats, and thieves, then he won't. It's kind of a flexible morality in high places. Here we're talking about a woman's life and who owns it, not a flexible issue.

Naturally there are a lot of folks worried about the life of the fetus and I can understand that, having worried about the same thing myself thirty-odd years ago. What bothers me about the picketers and the killers in this group is that they never offer to pay for raising the full-term baby. Now the mother herself may have some very good reasons of her own for seeking an abortion, that's none of our business, but if these pro-life people put up some real money to pay for raising the child, maybe the mother would change her mind.

This is really a no-brainer, but it does seem like the people who make the most trouble about abortion are the same people with their hands out: not giving, only taking, thank you. They don't offer charity, they make demands. I guess that's the reason the fourth estate calls this activity grassroots politics; they act just like the politicians.

The issue of abortion boils down to the question, who owns your life? Given that the state claims that ownership, given that individuals have repeatedly denied the state's claim for centuries, given that there has never been a resolution between the two claims, what is the truth?

Who owns your life?

FUN WITH NUMBERS

2001

After reading Christopher Westley's fine article, *The Carriage-Trade Trend*, http://www.mises.org/fullstory.asp?control=743 I got to thinking about the imminent demise of the health-care industry in this country. After earning my living in this business for thirty-eight years, I feel kind of attached to it, and I will be sorry to see it go. Why does this have to happen? I went looking for some facts and figures.

I wish that the private organizations of private businesses would collect and publish their own statistics. Apparently they let their "parent" organization, the federal government, do it for them. I'm sorry I had to resort to state sources, but there it is.

To explain the failure of this business, my own hypothesis is twofold; one, that the state won't pay for the obligation it has undertaken, and two, that the bulk of the money earmarked for health-care goes to pay for state mandated bureaucracies and not for health-care.

The first issue is pretty straightforward. Imagine that you could selectively decide to pay for only certain items on your auto mechanic's bill after the work was done. Imagine that the mechanic was forced to take what you paid without recourse to any system of justice. Imagine that it was the law. That's how it works. A full-time staff at the Medicare third-party-payer contractor's office, read insurance company, changes the billing rules and the billing codes willy-nilly. One day your electrocardiogram is paid, one day it isn't. The advisories fall like rain into the offices of health-care providers, who must necessarily employ a full-time staff to keep track of them. One little mistake in a multi-digit code means no money. But then they only pay a percentage of whatever charge they approve, so maybe you have to charge $1253.00 for a procedure to get $550.00 in your bank account, which, after you subtract wages, taxes, and the overhead of maintaining your own personal bureaucracy, means that you may end up with 10% of what you charged. This socialist reality drives some private practitioners into true private practice—cash only; others it drives out of the business altogether. (I don't think mechanics would like it either.)

To address the second issue, I asked myself this question: For every health-care professional, how many non-professional clerical workers are there in health-care related bureaucracies? I wanted to include and count everybody working in hospitals, clinics, DME offices, doctor's offices, city, state, and federal health-care offices, and third-party-payer insurance company offices, and then compare the numbers.

I searched for the numbers of people employed in 1960, five-years before Medicare, and for the numbers of people employed in 2000, thirty-five years after Medicare. Alas, I could not find these numbers. However, I did find some numbers that were pretty interesting.

In 1983, for example ftp://ftp.hrsa.gov/bhpr/nationalcenter/factbook/fb110.pdf, there were 6,888 "registered hospitals" in this country and 36,703 "administrators and assistant administrators". Ten years later, in 1993, there were 6,467 hospitals and 69,393 administrators. Say what? The number of hospitals declined and the number of administrators nearly doubled. It looks like an epidemic.

In the same time period, the number of Registered Nurses working in these hospitals went from 770,846 to 958,966. It appears that this modest increase in the number of nurses required a whopping increase in the number of administrators. Of course, there is no correlation between nurses and administrators; health-care cannot do without nurses. Bureaucracies just grow, it's what they do. (One hospital where I worked had twenty-nine managers for twenty-five patient beds.)

On the key issue of the growth rate in the number of clerical staff involved in getting medical bills paid or not paid, I nearly drew a blank. One source that had numbers ftp://146.142.4.23/pub/suppl/EMPSIT. CESEEB12.TXT declared that the number of people employed in 2000 in "Medical Service and Heath Insurance" was 381,000, and in "Hospital and Medical Service Plans" was 304,000. That means, I take it, that 685,000 people were employed as clerical workers by third-party-payer health insurance companies who contract their services to Medicare. Technically, they are not government employees, though in reality their paychecks come from taxes.

I could not find any numbers for insurance company employees prior to 2000, so I don't know their growth rate. I would really like to know how many pencil pushers worked for these outfits in 1960. I hope that somebody who knows will tell me.

So maybe I'm not much of a research kind of guy and I can't prove my hypothesis after all. But I do have a rule of thumb; I call it the parking-lot rule and you can prove it for yourself. Drive through any hospital parking lot on any day of the week and count the empty parking spaces. Then drive through on any weekend or holiday and count the empty parking spaces. You will see a marked difference. The difference is, the bureaucrats don't work on weekends. Count their numbers.

Previously published at http://www.lewrockwell.com

MORE FUN WITH NUMBERS

2002

In my first article on this subject, I tried to figure out the growth of the health-care bureaucracy compared to the growth of the health-care industry. This time I'd like to compare the numbers of people who have a financial interest in the redistribution of wealth fraud with the overall population, especially with the working population.

The 2000 census http://www.census.gov reported a total population of around 300 million; I say "around" because I know for a fact that they missed a few. Of that number, around 129 million http://www.bls.gov/oes/home.htm were employed, or about 43% of the total population. Interesting that the number of individual tax returns for 1999 <http://www.taxfoundation.org/prtopincometable.html> was 126 million, meaning either that the working population grew by 3 million people in one year or that 3 million working people didn't file a federal income tax return in 1999. Whatever, it appears that of all the working people in 2000, about 40 million people worked directly for political government at all levels, or about 31% of the total number of working people or 13% of the total population (see footnote).

Now you wouldn't think that a mere 13% of the population could command a livelihood from the majority 87% of the population, but they have two things in their favor. One, the legal use of force to collect taxes. Two, the tacit approval of the large number of people who share in the plunder.

I could not find numbers that counted the un-funded contingent liabilities of government, that is retirement for politicians, military and police personnel, and bureaucrats. Consequently, I took the population figure http://www.census.gov/govs/apes/00stlus.txt for people over the age of 62, assuming that all have a financial interest in the redistribution of wealth fraud. Here we have another 40 million people.

Whereas 13% of a population looks like the tail wagging the dog in society, 26% begins to look like something else, especially when we consider that this block on the receiving end is 47% of the total workforce and state dependents combined. Taxpayers should not be happy.

Please note that I am not counting the numbers of people who work for government contractors. Their incomes also derive from taxation and I cannot imagine (or find) their numbers, except in health-care ftp://146.142.4.23/pub/suppl/EMPSIT.CESEEB12.TXT.

Finally, I would like to introduce another curious set of numbers. In the 2000 election, about 100 million people voted. 200 million people did not vote. Surely, 200 million Americans were not too sick or too young to vote. Deducting whatever number you wish for the sick and for youth, there is still the massive secession from the political system to consider. And isn't it curious that the 100 million number of voters resembles the 80 million number of tax-dependents? Ah, maybe it's just a coincidence, but that's the fun with numbers..

Footnote:

http://www.bls.gov/oes/home.htm

Community and social services: 1,465,000
Education, training, and library: 7,450,960
Healthcare practitioners and technical: 6,041,210
Healthcare support: 3,039,430
Protective services: 3,009,070
Medical secretaries: 283,150

http://web1.whs.osd.mil/mmid/military/ms9.pdf

Active duty military personnel 2000: 2,944,228

http://web1.whs.osd.mil/mmid/civilian/fy2000/July2000/July00.htm

Civilians at DoD: 756,209

http://www.census.gov/govs/apes/00fedfun.txt

Federal government employment: 2,899,363

http://www.census.gov/govs/apes/00stlus.txt

State and local government employment: 15,077,703

Previously published at http://www.lewrockwell.com

Addendum: One possible conclusion that I did not spell out in this article derives from the observation that around 26% of our population lives on tax money, for a ratio of around 1.6 taxpayers to every tax receiver. People who live on tax money spend it in the economy just like the taxpayers do, which leads me to think that we are all to some extent co-dependents with the state in this massive churning of tax money in our society. I admit that the average Registered Nurse, for example, probably does not perceive that his income derives from taxes, though in large part it does, but when push comes to shove, he will not want Medicare reform to eliminate his job. We don't bite the hand that feeds us. This reality greatly inhibits truth seeking, and freedom of action. Tax churning thus represents an enormous hidden prop to political government. Now whether this came about accidentally over time, or whether it was a deliberate objective to the neo-mercantilists, the elite, over the past century is a question that I cannot reliably answer, yet it seems to fit in with their overall strategy to enslave world populations. It's something to think about.

I Wonder

2001

I wonder how many aspects of human life are not imaginary abstractions? Birth, death, food, and reproduction are not imaginary, I suppose, although much of what passes for thought in our minds is imaginary. However, it seems to take considerable effort to imagine something that has never existed before, like Leonardo da Vinci imagined his flying machine. I wonder what would have happened if somebody had imagined a useful connection between Archimedes' screw and the toy steam engines that entertained folks centuries before Christ. Maybe Julius would have become the founder of the Caesar Motor Company instead of becoming just another politician stabbed in the back by his buddies. But they had plenty of slaves to do the manual labor in those days and the idea of building a machine to do the work was plainly unimaginable.

I wonder what the odds are that a native male child born today in an Amazon rain forest would grow up to become an astronaut? Considering the short life expectancy, the high mortality rate, the endemic drug addiction, and the narrow focus of social life on internecine rivalries, it would seem that the odds are high against such a child acquiring the necessary imaginary abstraction of himself piloting a rocket to the moon. If he can't think of it, he can't do it.

I wonder why our ancient ancestors accepted the organizing principle of the sword and slavery as the only kind of government they could imagine? I wonder why this principle is still accepted by people living today? I suppose I should forgive the ancients for their lack of foresight, hindsight, or any insight at all into their repeated failures to create a durable society, because the use of physical force to get what we want is buried deep in our animal nature. I cannot forgive the people living today, however, since it is plain for all to see that the sword means extinction, and that our enslavement is nearly absolute. I wonder why we can't imagine a better way to do things?

I wonder what would have happened if people living in America and in Europe during the 1800s would have listened to the likes of Frederick Bastiat, Etienne de la Boetie, and Henry David Thoreau, and acted on their advice to mankind? What if France had become the first political jurisdiction in the history of mankind to suspend all meddling in the private affairs of individuals and businesses? What? No tariffs? What if France had instituted a cash and carry justice system? What? No taxes? Would America and England have lagged behind when the world's wealth began to pour into and out of France? Would this example have been ignored by Italy? Spain? Russia? Without tariffs in America, whence the Civil War? But of course, they didn't listen. Who could imagine what would happen if people ruled themselves one by one, and nobody was put in charge?

I wonder if we human beings have a genetic disposition for doing things that don't make sense? We have tried the sword and slavery model of political government over and over and over and it always fails, so we decide to try it again. We're kind of like the kid hunkered down in his rain forest hut, snorting dope and trying to dream up three ways to get even with his mother's cousin's nephew in the village downstream; we can't imagine anything else. I wonder what he'll wonder when the radioactive rain begins to fall?

Last, but not least, I wonder how many people have read *The Art of Community* by Spencer H. MacCallum (Institute for Humane Studies, Inc., 1970)? I finally stumbled across this book (http://www.laissezfaire-books.com) and read it recently. Mr. MacCallum is a good writer and a careful scholar who presents an imaginative alternative to political government without ever exactly saying that's what he's doing. Well, maybe that isn't what he intended to do, but that's what he's done, and it's no more mysterious in operation than your local shopping mall. It makes my wondering whirl.

Previously published at http://www.lewrockwell.com

MAKING SENSE

2002

Life generally made sense when I was growing up. We plowed the fields, planted the seed, and harvested the grain. We planted fruit trees, trimmed them, sprayed them, and harvested the fruit. We fed the cows and chickens and we got milk and eggs and meat in return. It made sense.

There was a large factory in town that built agricultural machinery. Steel was shipped in by train from the mills in Gary, Indiana, and then transformed into harvesters and hay balers and mowers and tractors. Most of the town's population worked there. I watched the long trainloads of shiny new machines shipped out to farmers all over the country. It made sense.

But some things didn't make sense. Government quotas and price supports on crops were first on my list of nonsense, with taxes running a close second. My dad was smart enough to figure out which crops to raise for cash, but he was only allowed raise so much. I could see that this tilted the market in favor of somebody else, though I didn't know who. I viewed taxes as just plain theft; why should we have to pay the county for the right to own and work the farm?

I got part of the answer to that question one summer when the bee inspector came around. We kept several hives of bees in different locations so they could pollinate the fruit trees and the crops and so we could harvest their honey. Any beekeeper knows when his hive is sick, so I didn't know why the hives had to be inspected by a stranger, but every year this guy showed up. Finally, one year, I noticed the county sticker on his car. I had met my first bureaucrat.

That was fifty years ago. Life stopped making sense to me shortly thereafter. Whereas I firmly believed that in order to get something useful, like money, a person had to do something useful, like work, I began to learn that a person could get something useful without doing anything useful at all. But early impressions are hard to shake.

I started working in a 200 bed hospital while I was in college in 1963. I was hired by the hospital administrator, who was also the director of nursing and the purchasing agent (she shared an office with the accounting lady). I did the job, I got paid. I understood that my income derived from fees charged by the hospital to patients who used the service; they either paid directly or their insurance paid for them.

When Medicare went into effect in 1965 the hospital business immediately doubled and the administrative staff quadrupled. I understood that my income still derived from fees for service, though much of it now came from Medicare taxes.

Administrative staff in hospitals never stopped growing and new hospitals went up everywhere, financed on government-backed, that is tax-based, loans. Medicare contractors, the insurance companies, expanded their bureaucracies as well. By 1985 the system was bankrupt, so Congress changed Medicare. No more fee for service. Where was my income coming from now?

In 1985 my profession went from being a major money-maker for hospitals to being a major money-loser for hospitals. Medicare pays for nothing that I do, but Medicare still requires hospitals to employ me (my profession). What does that make me? A working welfare recipient?

Socialized medicine doesn't make sense, but then neither does (anti)Social (in)Security or the Patriot Act or American Imperialism. Nothing emanating from the District of Criminals makes sense, unless you happen to be one of them. Their tentacles spread everywhere, into every business and into our personal lives, stealing our privacy and our dignity, as well as our money. They threaten us and they spy on us, then they tell us to spy on each other. It doesn't make sense.

I wish I'd run that bee inspector off the farm with a shotgun when the world still made sense to me.

Previously published at http://www.lewrockwell.com

Intellectual Property

2001

Considering an issue from the point of view of the state is fraught with hazard. We must beware of their definitions and of the twists and turns of their context, for their objective is not truth and justice, but control and power. We are much safer to consider an issue from our own observations of reality, and by using a process of logical analysis that leads to conclusions that don't need to be enforced with a gun. The issue of intellectual property is one that calls for great care and clarity, for we are dealing here with the contents of our minds, which the state would very much like to control.

The Intellectual Property Reference Library defines intellectual property http://myweb.servtech.com/public/mbobb/glossary/gloss_i.htm as "intangible creations of the mind, such as inventions." I take that to mean new ideas. To distinguish new ideas from old ideas, I will also call new ideas innovations. Hence intellectual property, new ideas, and innovations all mean "intangible creations of the mind" in this essay.

Where do ideas come from? Since ideas themselves do not occur in nature as independently existing objects, like apples hanging on a tree, ideas are necessarily a creation of the human mind. I will not address the question of whether life forms other than Homo Sapiens have ideas of their own, because we cannot reliably communicate with them and we don't know for sure. I will also not address the question of whether ideas exist at all; those who wish to use their ideas to prove the non-existence of their ideas are welcome to chase their tails as they wish. From simple observation of everyday human life, we do know for sure that ideas exist in the human mind, and that ideas can be communicated from one human mind to another. But that observation does not answer the question, where do ideas come from?

It would be convenient to believe that babies were born with a set of ideas hard-wired into their brains and nervous systems that immediately ensured their survival. Observation quickly tells us that this is not true. Human babies cannot get up and move about at birth and they have no idea what is nutritious or safe to eat until some person teaches them. Ideas are either learned or discovered. Ideas already learned by one person and stored in that person's mind as knowledge can be communicated to another person in a variety of ways, including direct example and the exchange of symbolic representations. Observing a baby learn to eat, to walk, and to speak a language instructs us in the process.

Our species in general tends to store ideas as knowledge in symbolic representation and then we pass along that knowledge from generation to generation. Some knowledge has proved to be vital to our species' survival, like knowing how to hunt and gather food that is not poisonous, and knowing how to build shelters and start fires. Some knowledge has proved to be threatening to our survival, like knowing how to lie, cheat, steal, rape, kill, and enslave. Some knowledge is false, like knowing the Earth is flat, stars are pinned to the ceiling, and pi is equal to three. Adult members of our species must evaluate the knowledge they intend to pass along for its usefulness and its validity, lest harmful or false knowledge brings future generations to calamity.

Looking at the characteristics of ideas as knowledge, however, does not reveal where ideas come from. Let's see where the idea of pi <http://www-groups.dcs.st-and.ac.uk/~history/HistTopics/Pi_through_the_ages.html> came from. Pi is the ratio between the circumference of a circle to its diameter. If we measure the distance around a circle, we will find that it is always the sum of three diameters plus a little bit more. We can use any measuring units at all, feet, meters, cubits, or just a piece of string without units, and it's always the same. We could measure it on the Moon, on Mars, on a spaceship, anywhere at all, and it's always the same: three and a little bit more. So what? Why is it important?

If we want to build something really big that won't fall down, we suddenly discover that we must know the value of pi in order to design it. Thus it comes as no surprise that the search for pi began in Babylon and in Egypt about one-hundred and sixty generations ago, when those people wanted to build some really big cities and tombs. The name of the person who initiated the search for pi in those days is not known to me. Archimedes of Syracuse, Sicily, http://www-groups.dcs.st-and.ac.uk/~history/Mathematicians/Archimedes.html discovered a value for pi very close to our own about ninety generations ago. Pi was discovered independently in China by Tsu Ch'ung Chi http://www-groups.dcs.st-and.ac.uk/~history/Mathematicians/Tsu.html eighteen generations ago. The history of pi is well documented from these early discoveries to the present time.

Parenthetically, it is of some interest to note that the Indiana House of Representatives unanimously passed a bill to change pi to three in 1897 http://www.urbanlegends.com/legal/pi_indiana.html. Fortunately, the Indiana Senate defeated it or future generations would have paid dearly for their hubris, that is, by laughing themselves to death. The laws of nature are not subject to revision by the laws of man.

Ideas come from the human mind. Some ideas, like pi, come from a human mind observing and interpreting facts in nature. An individual human person's ideas are stored as electro-chemical synapses in that individual person's brain. An individual person may acquire ideas from other persons, even long-dead persons, and communicate ideas to other persons in a variety of ways familiar to us all. When an individual person's brain dies or otherwise ceases to function, the ideas in that person's brain cease to exist; at least there is no reliable observational evidence to the contrary as yet.

New ideas, innovations, derive from old ideas. New ideas do not spring into existence in an intellectual vacuum. Babies do not announce the mathematical equation for the unified field theory when they are born. First they must learn to understand the language of mathematics and the entire body of knowledge that we call physics, a formidable collection of old ideas. Then they may extrapolate from the old to something entirely new, an "intangible creation of the mind," an innovation.

I take it as a fact in nature that my brain is mine. I mean, precisely, that my brain is not another person's brain, but is mine. My brain exists inside my skull, not inside another person's skull. From that I infer that the contents of my brain are also mine, that is, the contents of my brain are not simultaneously the contents of another person's brain. Some of the contents of my brain are old ideas that I have learned from other people. Learning ideas from other people does not subtract ideas from their brains; in fact, their brains may be long dead and turned into dust. From these old ideas I may extrapolate to new ideas. Now the question is, are these new ideas mine? To put it otherwise, do these new ideas belong to some other person? If these new ideas exist in my brain alone and in the brain of no other person, how can they belong to another person? They can't, unless I choose to communicate them to another person. When my new ideas become lodged in another person's brain, then they belong to the other person, as surely as they still belong to me. Thus intellectual property can belong to a whole host of people at the same time for generation after generation, but let's not forget that the new ideas began with one person and originally belonged solely to that person. Does this make any difference?

I would like to illustrate this with a simple question. How long did it take Julius Caesar to fly from Gaul to Rome? Stupid question. There is no answer to this question because no man on Earth could fly anywhere until the Wright Brothers invented the self-powered, heavier-than-air flying machine nearly eighty generations later. Were the Romans too stupid to invent the airplane? I doubt it. The Romans lacked knowledge crucial to such an innovation, new ideas that would not be discovered and disseminated for centuries. Why the Romans did not seek to discover such knowledge is a good question, but the fact remains that they did not have the knowledge and therefore they could not fly even if they had wanted to fly. For us, the Wright Brothers have made a world of difference. And here is the crux of the modern issue. Did the Wright Brothers have any rights associated with their intellectual property? Did they own their innovations?

Let's pause in the investigation here and consider for a moment the profound difficulties that surround intellectual property. Archimedes bristled at the folks who claimed his discoveries were their discoveries; he even set a trap for them by publishing false theorems for them to claim. Newton became so distressed at false claims of priority that he vowed to renounce natural philosophy altogether, which he did. The Wright Brothers wasted the better part of both of their lifetimes in futile legal defense of their patented inventions. These are only three small examples among thousands; there is clearly a problem here, although people who are not innovators don't recognize it. This is an observational reality to keep in mind as we continue.

Now we enter the murky world of political government, where reality in nature is defied by legal, codified lying, cheating, stealing, and killing. The first principle of the state is, everything belongs to the state. Native Americans had a problem with this principle after European states declared that they owned the land in America and nobody could use it without their express permission. Land grants, or patents, were made to crown favorites in exchange for future plunder from the work of colonists, indentured servants, and outright slaves. These so-called quit-rents were stolen from the grantees at the point of a gun, just as property taxes are extorted from citizens today. Rebels were murdered. Imports and exports were minutely regulated and smuggling flourished. Seventeenth Century America <http://www.mises.org/product.asp?sku=B268> was not a nice place to live, but it was still better than living in Europe.

The American colonial period is riddled with fluctuating laws that favored the crown one minute and favored the colonists the next. Nobody was ignorant of the stakes in the game. Just like today, states want the wealth and states will murder to get it, but states can't murder everybody or the game is over, so a constant process of negotiation, including terrorism on both sides, ensues. In the traditional game, the wealth in question consists of tangible property, like land and money, raw materials, agricultural and manufactured products, i.e., things that can be recorded and stolen. The IRS wants the real stuff, not a bunch of airy-fairy ideas.

The state treats intellectual property like a thing, a tangible thing. On March 3, 1876, two men visited the U.S. Patent Office with nearly identical inventions. The first was Alexander Graham Bell, the second was Elisha Gray http://www.geog.buffalo.edu/Geo666/flammger/tele2.html. We know the outcome: one of the largest state-protected monopolies in history was born. When the state speaks about fostering competition, it is competition for the state's favor they are talking about.

When the state grants monopoly privileges to an innovation, the state is acting on the presumption that they own the innovator, the innovation, the consumer, and all subsequent wealth that results. Like any criminal organization, the state arrogates this power to itself with a gun. There is no rational reason in the universe why Gray, Bell, Edison, and a host of other innovators could not have gone into the telephone business as direct competitors and let the consumer decide which one provided the best service. This nonsense continues today, with committees of bureaucrats who do not comprehend the technology arguing about whom to permit to do what. Their fundamental presumption is false. The state does not own the innovator, the innovation, the consumer, or the subsequent wealth that is produced. To verify that this is true, let the state suspend its threat of force for five years and call its laws guidelines only, then see what happens in the world of innovation.

Copyright is no better. I personally use the word on documents that I write to formally declare that I wrote them; I would prefer to use my PGP <http://www.pgpi.org/> signature and I will as soon as we quit fooling around with paper and ink reproductions. Perhaps the worst effect of patents and copyrights is that they give the innovator a false sense of security, so the innovator does not seek true security. One of the easiest ways to steal intellectual property is from the patent office; perhaps the greatest technical innovator in history, Nicola Tesla, http://www.sjsu.edu/depts/Museum/tesla.html was ruined by this means. Now, just for the sake of argument, and with sincere apologies to Ayn Rand, let's say that I self-publish a comic book called "Atlas Slugged" featuring the heroic adventures of John Glut, idiot savant, and Dimi Frank, frigid beauty. Who cares? I mean, I know that some folks would care, all right, but all things considered, who would bother to read such a farce? How could I even market it? Word could go around the planet on the Internet in a hot minute and my reputation would be dust forever. At present, of course, the state would serve a cease and desist order, halt publication, and drag me into court for plagiarism and defamation of trademarks and then take everything I own, all at taxpayers expense, and give me a perfect excuse to market the thing underground. In some socialist havens of yesteryear, writers were even murdered under the assumption that this kind of "thing" could be stopped. A writer can be buried, his ideas cannot.

Innovators do have a problem. How do they get paid? This is such a big problem that many people say it is not a problem at all; in other words, they can't think about it. Other people, even libertarians, believe firmly in the intellectual communism of the "public" library or, today, the Internet, without regard to the contradiction inherent in both. Despite the protests, or the silence, of people on this issue, the observational fact remains that new ideas originate in a single mind and if that new idea is worth anything, that single mind should get paid for it. Ayn Rand herself, of all people, objected to this idea in *The Objectivist Newsletter*, Volume 13, Number 5, May, 1964, where she staunchly defended our patent and copyright state. By the way, I am most amused to discover that this essay is not on-line, a pragmatic contradiction of her argument. The problem remains, however unseen, unacknowledged, or unspoken it may be.

How can an innovator protect intellectual property? Patents and copyrights are not granted by the state with insurance or a money-back-guarantee. Disputes are not settled in private arbitration between proprietarily interested parties who are all insured and guaranteed, they are settled in open court by parties whose sole interest is the ticking of the clock. Some software innovators have come up with an elegant solution to their problem of reverse engineering a program; they might have learned this one from Archimedes. They build in a trap. Reverse engineering will destroy the program. Hardware innovators have a difficult problem and I don't know if they can solve it by a similar method; they might start thinking along those lines, however, instead of depending on the state. Going one step further, there is clearly a wide-open market for the protection of intellectual property and I believe it's only a matter of time before new social mechanisms emerge to do just that without the state. We need some innovation here. We need to replace the state.

INSPIRATION

2002

I am fond of beautiful things. I have a small collection of replicas that I like to look at and to think about. The statue of David http://www.anthroarcheart.org/tblm36.htm reminds me of the beauty of the male body and of resolute defiance in the face of the enemy; it also reminds me of Michelangelo, the man who created this sculpture over four-hundred years ago. The statue of the Winged Victory http://www.artchive.com/artchive/G/greek/winged_victory.jpg.htm l reminds me of the beauty of the female body and of resolute courage in the face of nature's storms; it also reminds me of a lost civilization that appreciated such things over two-thousand years ago. These things inspire in me a vision of mankind that is positive, virtuous, graceful, and strong. I like that vision.

Where does one go to find inspiration in the everyday world around us? I find it right in front of my face as I type these words: the personal computer and the Internet. These things came out of the human mind into a civilization that appreciated such things in my own lifetime. Thus I find that high-technology and the science that goes into it are equally as inspiring as fine art, classical music, and great literature. This is the kind of world I want for myself and for my children.

A close friend sent me this work of art <http://antwrp.gsfc.nasa.gov /apod/image/0011/earthlights_dmsp_big.jpg>. It is a NASA composite photograph of the Earth with the lights on at night. I was stunned by the beauty of the photo and everything it implies. My first thought was, "If only Nichola Tesla <http://www.newton.mec.edu/brown/te/INVEN-TORS/INVENTORS/byKIDS/alber.html> could see this." My second thought was, "This was impossible a century ago." Earth was a dark place at night for all of the millennia of mankind's history until Michael Faraday <http://www.phy.hr/~dpaar/fizicari/xfaraday.html> and James Clark Maxwell <http://www.studyworld.com/james_clark_maxwell.htm> laid the theoretical and experimental groundwork in the Nineteenth Century that led to Tesla's alternating current generator in the Twentieth.

We might pause here for a moment to consider these origins of what we call electricity. There was no Disraeli extolling the benefits of electricity to a Queen Victoria while the knowledge was being developed under their noses. Governments did not invent electricity, governments merely stole control of it after private individuals created it. Nineteenth Century mercantilism still infects this industry.

I studied this photograph for hours, picking out the cities around the globe and finding explanations for the dark areas. Some are obvious, like the Sahara Desert, the Arctic, and Antarctic, while some are less obvious, like central Africa. The Dark Continent is still dark because political governments there keep it dark. With that thought in mind, I scrolled across the photograph to look at California.

The California energy crisis has not gone away. The producers of electricity are still separated from the consumers of electricity by miles of red tape generated by tax-supported bureaucrats at the command of tax-supported politicians. Residents of the Silicon Valley, arguably the most technologically advanced population on Earth, are still at the mercy of some dimwit in Sacramento who can order a blackout in San Jose and Los Gatos to benefit some peculiar friends in San Francisco. This has happened before and it will happen again.

I contemplate this photograph with a mixture of pride in the creativity of our species and sadness in our faults as a species. What took Michelangelo three years of hard work could be turned into a dozen meaningless chunks of marble in three minutes by fanatic vandals or vicious morons. What took the dedicated hard work of millions of people for a century could be plunged into the darkness of the ages once again by the same fanatics or morons. Our splendid space-age technology is still ruled by our Dark Age political governments.

I am fond of beautiful things. This beautiful photograph inspires me to think that it's time for a change in the way we do things.

Previously published at http://www.lewrockwell.com

Conceived In Liberty

A Review

2002

Introduction

Conceived in Liberty by Murray N. Rothbard was first published in 1975 by Arlington House, Publishers. In 1999 it was republished and copy-righted by the Ludwig von Mises Institute. In a detailed narrative well supported by period documents as well as historical interpretation, Rothbard describes the European settlement of the North American continent from its beginning in 1564 to the post-revolutionary confederation of states in 1784. Rothbard writes from an explicitly libertarian point of view; thus, in Volume IV (pg.237) he states:

"The polar opposites in political regimes were slavery on the one hand, and self-government on the other, and self-government or self-direction was the key to liberty, not government by law, since laws can be and are made by one person or set of persons to bind others."

The conflict between these "polar opposites" is the timeless theme of this work.

Volume I: A New Land, A New People: The American Colonies In The Seventeenth Century.

European adventurers in the Holy Land discovered pepper and silk from the orient and the race was on. Soon all of the European maritime countries were exploring the oceans to find a way to get these luxuries. Then Columbus bumped into an island.

European countries staked a claim on the new continent without consulting the native population, who had no notion of property in real estate, then the royal bureaucrats parceled out the land to royal favorites, including themselves. The feudal model of society and government was exported along with the colonists who were supposed to develop the wilderness in the name of their monarch. To accomplish the hard physical work entailed in that development, slaves were demanded. Call them what you will, serfs, peasants, yeomen, indentured servants, the first people who cleared the forests and plowed and planted and harvested were white slaves exported from their European homeland in servitude to their masters and to their states. And they were not happy about it. Rothbard dramatically details the intense and relentless conflicts between masters and slaves in every colony.

Religious fanaticism contributed no small part to the misery and, in addition, confused the issue in many places, especially in the Puritan colonies where religious leaders were also temporal masters. I was shocked and horrified by what the people had to endure, which is a tribute to the skill of the writer as well as a condemnation of what actually happened.

The absolute evil of the enslavement of African people also arose during this century and grew as the colonies grew. There were slave markets in all of the major cities, north and south, while the financial gains went primarily to British, Dutch, and New England shipping magnates. Few people remarked the contradiction inherent in the Christian slave trade; speaking against it was a dangerous thing to do.

The truly remarkable and nearly unbelievable thing that occurred in Seventeenth Century America was the settlement of Pennsylvania by the pacifist Quakers. They denounced slavery and they renounced the use of force and, once arrived, they ignored their royal master, paid no taxes, bought their land from the Indians, and worked industriously for their own individual purposes. They enjoyed twenty years of utter anarchy! But they were brought to heel in the end.

Less remarkable, but more significant for future events, was the emergence of Rhode Island as an unauthorized colony in the midst of royal estates. It became a refuge for political and religious dissidents and a defiant harbor of free trade.

Volume II: "Salutary Neglect": The American Colonies In The First Half Of The Eighteenth Century.

England emerged as the dominant imperialist force in America after defeating France and Spain in war, and although the British Parliament passed laws aimed at fleecing the colonists, these laws were poorly enforced, a deliberate Whig policy called "Salutary Neglect." Trade flourished between America, Europe, and the West Indies, as well as between the colonies themselves. Differences between the colonies gradually disappeared as common forms of local government and common experiences among the colonists brought people together. Moreover, the works of Isaac Newton and John Locke were becoming ever more popular in England as well as America, arousing a new spirit of rational inquiry into the laws of nature and the nature of man.

Harmonious settlement was continually disrupted, however, by conflicts between the settlers and their appointed masters. European immigrants poured into the wilderness and carved out homesteads for themselves, only to discover that powerful officials had claims on the land and assumed claims on their persons and property. Many forms of taxation were devised, and resisted. Southern governors suppressed slave rebellions, while northern governors suppressed sedition and tax evasion.

The British Tory war party initiated a new war against France by mid-century. In America it became known as the French and Indian War and it was, Rothbard points out, a deliberate land-grab. The British emerged victorious and the Tories swept the Whigs from office. Rothbard concludes Volume II on this note (pg.268):

"Enjoying the blessings of Salutary neglect, the American colonies had been able, in the first half of the eighteenth century, to ignore the *de jure* mercantilist restrictions and edicts of Great Britain and to flourish in virtual *de facto* independence from the mother country. It was high time, the British imperialists felt, to cast off the restrictions of salutary neglect and to bring the American colonies to heel."

Volume III: Advance To Revolution, 1760–1775

The British boot came down hard; the Crown wanted its loot. Stern new laws restricting and taxing imports, exports, and manufacturing were imposed and more or less obeyed. Then, in 1765, Parliament passed the Stamp Act.

This was a sinister threat indeed, for it required that all documents, from a bill of sale to a marriage license, be written on specially stamped paper available only from British agents. Americans were aghast at the prospect, but did not know how to respond. There did not seem to be any way around it.

Then a young lawyer in the Virginia House of Burgesses by the name of Patrick Henry made an impassioned speech calling for resolutions to protest the law. Seven "Virginia Resolves" were drafted by Henry and his group of young radicals, each one more defiant than the one before. Conservatives defeated the sixth and seventh and, behind Henry's back, repealed the fifth, but all seven were published in newspapers elsewhere as if they had been passed. Rothbard writes (pg.102):

"But if most people were awakened and stirred by Henry and Virginia, who would lead them? *For the masses cannot act without some form of organization and articulate leadership."* (Emphasis mine)

"No help, of course, could be expected from the arch Tory and opportunist, Benjamin Franklin."

He continues (Pg.104): "In the early summer of 1765, Sam Adams gathered together a group of Bostonians to lead and direct the people in the streets." What ensued was no less than a mini-revolution where masses of people rose up against the British Stamp *agents* throughout the colonies and forced them to resign their royal posts. It was a brilliant strategy, and it worked; British ships were not allowed to land the stamped paper. After much political wrangling, Parliament repealed the Stamp Act the following March.

The success of united action brought Americans closer together than ever before, while in England it encouraged the people at the same time that it infuriated the Tories and George III. That fury resulted in the Townshed Acts of 1767 which "imposed new import duties on glass, lead, paint, paper, and tea." (pg.166) "As a companion to the new duties, another Townshed Act radically increased the enforcement powers of British officialdom." (pg.167)

The American response was to organize a colony-wide boycott of British imports. Organizing the colonies to agree to this boycott was no easy task, but it was done, and it worked. All but one of the Townshed Acts was repealed in 1770. The one that remained was the tax on tea.

The British Crown tried to accomplish two things. One, to bail out their own bankrupt creature, the East India Company, and two, once again, to plunder the American colonists. The tax was modest and could have easily been paid. What the Americans feared was encroachment by the East India Company, a state monopoly backed up by the British Army. Rothbard writes (pg.263):

"Defense of one's property and commerce against a privileged monopoly is *required* by libertarian principle. Liberty *implies* property rights and free trade; it does not contradict them." (Emphasis his.)

The previous revolts had resulted in the formation of the armed Sons of Liberty and the extra-legal Committees of Correspondence, so the colonies had a proto-army and efficient communications. They were unable to convince the designated consignees to refuse the tea shipments. Three ships arrived in Boston harbor, but the radicals patrolled the docks and the ships could not unload. The royal governor planned to seize the ships and unload them with the troops. Time was running out. On December 16, 1773, "a great mass meeting of the 'body' of eight thousand people learned of Hutchinson's refusal to allow the *Dartmouth* to sail home." (pg.267) "The prominent merchant John Rowe asked meaningfully, 'Who knows how tea will mingle with salt water?'" (pg.267)

"Thereupon, a remarkably disciplined ginger group of Sons of Liberty, disguised as Mohawk Indians, rushed to Griffin's Wharf, boarded all three tea ships, and spent several hours of the night dumping every bit of East India tea into Boston Harbor." (pg.267)

British government was horrified, British people were delighted. "The Crown called Parliament into session in early March 1774 and presented a series of four Coercive Acts designed to bring Britain's might to bear upon Boston." (pg.273) The Coercive Acts closed the port of Boston, established a royal counsel in Massachusetts and barred town meetings, exempted royal officials from high crimes, and quartered British troops on the people. An army of occupation would put an end to colonial resistance once and for all.

"The embattled colonists, sharpened and increasingly unified by the years of struggle for liberty against Great Britain, hastened to accept that challenge." (pg.279) The Committees of Correspondence got busy. "On September 5, 1774, there met at Philadelphia the most fateful and momentous assemblage ever gathered in the colonies: the Continental Congress." (pg.296) They decided to reinstate the boycott on all imported British goods.

On April 18, 1775, General Gage sent a troop of infantry to capture Sam Adams and John Hancock and a rebel supply dump in Concord. He expected little opposition. The troop met John Parker and seventy minutemen at Lexington. Shots rang out and the Americans fell. The British troop went on to Concord. "While the British were destroying the remaining stores, three to four hundred militiamen gathered at the bridge into Concord and advanced on the British rear guard." (pg.328) They drove the British off the bridge. The tumult attracted more and more Americans to the fight. The British return to Boston became a nightmare. "Events could not have gone better for the American cause: initial aggression and massacre by the arrogant redcoats, then turned into utter rout by the aroused and angry people of Massachusetts." (pg.329)

The American Revolution had begun.

Volume IV: The Revolutionary War, 1775–1784

The Second Continental Congress met on May 10 and here the ultimate fate of America would begin to take form. The heart of every particular issue that faced this Congress over the next decade was whether to allow people to run their own affairs, or to rule them in the time honored master-slave political model. War was at hand. Conservatives wanted to ignore the popular uprising in Massachusetts and appeal to the Crown for compromise; radicals wanted to support the uprising. Rothbard writes (pg.32):

"Here the Massachusetts radicals were in a cruel dilemma; any army under the Continental Congress would mean, in contrast to a guerrilla army, the inevitable buildup of central state apparatus, and of a highly expensive and burdensome state army, which would inevitably saddle all Americans with heavy taxes, inflation, and debt."

Congress chose to establish an army. Further wrangling between conservatives and radicals led to the appointment of George Washington to lead that army; Washington, although militarily inept and unqualified, was both an arch conservative and a radical, like most of the Virginia oligarchy, and was chosen as a political compromise.

Rothbard makes clear that the colonies were by no means united in purpose at this point. Americans were willing to fight against British coercion, but many, if not most, saw themselves as British subjects fighting unjust laws; remove the laws, as before, and they would become peaceful subjects once more. "Furthermore, the old and obsolete Whig ideal of virtual independence under a figurehead king of both Britain and America could only be shattered if the king were to be attacked personally." (pg.135) The man who did so was Thomas Paine.

Paine had exceptionally clear insight into what was happening in America. Self-educated, working class, and already middle-aged, he arrived in Philadelphia in 1774 and went to work for a printer. He published a pamphlet denouncing slavery the following year. "Lexington and Concord moved Paine to turn his talents to the radical revolutionary cause." (pg.136) Then, in January of 1776, Paine published his *Common Sense*. "Tom Paine had, at a single blow, become the voice of the American Revolution and the greatest single force in propelling it to completion and independence." (pg.137)

"On June 7, in happy obedience to the instructions resolved by Virginia on May 15, Richard Henry Lee submitted to the Continental Congress a momentous resolution for the independence of the United Colonies." (pg.175) For once the Congress agreed and the committee to draft such a declaration was appointed on June 11. Thus the Declaration of Independence was completed and approved by Congress on July 4, 1776.

Meanwhile, the war was heating up. "The mighty British invasion force began to assemble off New York City in late June, 1776. It was headed by the Howe brothers, Gen. Sir William Howe in charge of land forces and his brother Admiral Richard Lord Howe, newly appointed overall commander-in-chief of the American theater." (pg.187)

George Washington with 19,000 militia stood opposed to 32,000 redcoats and 10,000 seamen. "If the British commanders had applied even moderate intelligence or devotion to their task, they could probably have wiped out Washington's army then and there and perhaps won the war on the spot." (pg.188) But they didn't, and historians still wonder why. Was it because the Howe brothers were Whigs and therefore sympathetic to the American cause? Washington amply demonstrated his incompetence while the Howe brothers dithered and chased him around and finally allowed his army to escape.

While the war erupted in sporadic campaigns, the battle for power in Congress continued unabated. Rothbard describes the struggle (pg.244):

"And what of the revolutionary radical principle of locating sovereignty in the people themselves rather than in the 'legitimate' government? Would not this be an insuperable barrier to the Right? But here the able conservatives proved shrewd indeed; they managed to drop quickly the belief in the sovereignty of the crown, and demagogically to incorporate the radical doctrine of popular sovereignty for their own ends. Indeed, they cynically appeared to be *more* democratic than the radicals; for they argued that only a strong national government could *really* represent all the people." (Emphasis his) And here the fraud of democratic government was born.

The Articles of Confederation passed by the Continental Congress in 1777 contradicted the Declaration of Independence, and so the libertarian cause was lost before it had hardly begun. The conservatives, led by the landed aristocracies, the traditional oligarchs of north and south, got what they wanted, a powerful central government designed to protect their financial interests. The radicals were conceded some rights for the common people as a sop to popular sentiment, all knowing that it would pose no threat to power in the long run.

The British, unable to pin down Washington's army, and constantly harassed by spontaneous eruptions of militia in the north, changed their strategy to an all out attack on the southernmost colony, Georgia. They expected to enlist local Tory supporters and then march north, conquering the colonies one by one. They took the coastal region easily, but they once again overestimated Tory support and underestimated local militia resistance. In addition, both France and Spain had declared war on Great Britain, which divided British attention and manpower.

The final battle in the war ended at Yorktown on October 19, 1781. The French fleet bombarded the city from the sea while the American forces bombarded the city from land. The British surrendered. Rothbard summarizes (pg.365):

"And so the revolutionary United States of America threw off the British yoke and won the first successful war of national liberation against western imperialism. Many factors entered into the victory, but the most important was the firm support for the war by the great majority of the American people. It was that support which harassed, enveloped, and finally destroyed the proud British armies come to conquer and occupy in the name of traditionally legitimate government. It was a revolution fueled by fervent belief in libertarian natural rights ideology and by cumulative reaction to growing British infringement on those rights, political, constitutional, and economic. Its victory was essentially a people's victory, of guerrilla strategy in its broadest sense: not only of the small, mobile guerrilla bands of the Marions and the Sumters, but also of ephemeral and suddenly appearing militia who largely fought in their own neighborhoods and on their own terrain."

Conclusion

This is history written at its finest. Murray Rothbard is a powerful writer, yet his text is as easy to read as any skillfully written fiction. Indeed, some of the events he describes seem as strange as fiction. I come away from this work with a sense that Rothbard wrote with glee, that he might have been laughing when he slapped down yet another historical myth; certainly he never failed to entertain me.

On the subject matter itself, I am sad to see that what was so nearly won was so completely lost.

Previously published at http://www.lewrockwell.com

ÉTIENNE DE LA BOÉTIE:

A Review

2001

While reading Carl Watner's fine collection of essays, *I Must Speak Out,* http://members.aol.com/vlntryst/imso.html, I became engrossed in Murray N. Rothbard's 1987 article entitled, "The Political Thought of Étienne de la Boétie." I couldn't believe it, so I read it again. Where have I been sleeping all these years? Why haven't I heard of Etienne de la Boetie before? Just on the off chance that some of you may have missed him http://www.bartleby.com/65/la/LaBoetie.html too, I'd like to call attention to him again.

La Boetie was born in France in 1530. Copernicus and Martin Luther were still living at the time and Francois I was King. He wrote his little treatise on government sometime in the 1550s. He died in 1563.

Rothbard was struck by the man's youthful genius and by the clarity of his thinking. He saw him as a harbinger of libertarian thinking to come. I fully agree and I recommend reading Rothbard's article. I was also struck by something else and I would like to put a short quotation in here to illustrate what I mean.

The Politics of Obedience:
The Discourse of Voluntary Servitude
http://www.blancmange.net/tmh/articles/laboetie.html
by Étienne de la Boétie

"It is indeed the nature of the populace, whose density is always greater in the cities, to be suspicious toward one who has their welfare at heart, and gullible toward one who fools them. Do not imagine that there is any bird more easily caught by decoy, nor any fish sooner fixed on the hook by wormy bait, than are all these poor fools neatly tricked into servitude by the slightest feather passed, so to speak, before their mouths. Truly it is a marvelous thing that they let themselves be caught so quickly at the slightest tickling of their fancy. Plays, farces, spectacles, gladiators, strange beasts, medals, pictures, and other such opiates, these were for ancient peoples the bait toward slavery, the price of their liberty, the instruments of tyranny."

Bread and circuses. Americans would laugh at the idea that they could be duped into slavery by such trivia. Americans are much too smart for that. Besides, we have television and movies and stereo surround-sound, we don't need the Emperor to entertain us. That's true, but we do believe we need other things, like courts and cops, the Pentagon, Social Security, Medicare, Medicaid, and all of the alphabet-soup agencies, the IRS, CIA, FBI, NSA, BATF, FCC, on and on.

Americans want the good life and there is no fault in that. I too want indoor plumbing, central air and heat, a microwave oven, car, refrigerator, television, computer, privacy, and safe streets like everybody else. It's the way we live. But is there a price on the good life that we refuse to see? And is this price our liberty?

La Boetie in the Sixteenth Century pointed out the hidden cost of political government. As long as we believe that the things we want come by benevolent kindness from the state, then we quietly acquiesce to various demands from the state and the price keeps going up. The state speaks eloquently about tax-cuts and moves us to cheers, but the taxes keep going up. The state does not speak about average families who must buy food and medication on credit because their wages are gone in Social Security and Medicare and sales taxes and income taxes and fees paid for permission from the state to eat or drink or drive around. The state does not speak about the source of the soaring cost of health-care, the result of bureaucratic micro-mismanagement put in place by the state itself. La Boetie called us fools. Indeed, we are. We look longingly for the day we can have our good life and our Social Security check too without working for it anymore. Free lunch! Bread and circuses for all!

"By these practices and enticements the ancient dictators so successfully lulled their subjects under the yoke, that the stupefied peoples, fascinated by the pastimes and vain pleasures flashed before their eyes, learned subservience as naively, but not so creditably, as little children learn to read by looking at bright picture books."

The problem is, socialism by any name doesn't work for very long. People lose incentive and begin to look for hand-outs from their state rather than take care of themselves. La Boetie wrote:

"Roman tyrants invented a further refinement. They often provided the city wards with feasts to cajole the rabble, always more readily tempted by the pleasure of eating than by anything else. The most intelligent and understanding amongst them would not have quit his soup bowl to recover the liberty of the Republic of Plato."

While meditating briefly on the meaning of life this morning, as I do every morning, I happened to glance down at my reading table and I saw a photograph of a group of my peers all dressed in the tee-shirt of a powerful political interest group. The ladies all looked so lovely in their tightly-permed silver hair and the men so handsome and proud, though bald, like me. But their mouths were tightly drawn, not smiling, and their fists clenched and arms raised in anger. Not so good for blood pressure, I thought, what are these people doing? I read the article. Ah, they demand more! More of everything! And they want the state to give it to them!

"The fools did not realize that they were merely recovering a portion of their own property, and that their ruler could not have given them what they were receiving without having first taken it from them."

La Boetie knew what he was talking about. Have we, the human race, learned nothing about the nature of human government in the last four-hundred and fifty years? Have we not repeated the mistakes of our ancestors over and over and over? Our science and our technology have thrust our species into an entirely new social environment, unprecedented in human history, and still we beg the state for bread and circuses while the state crushes us with its rules and taxes. Do we really need the state?

La Boetie may be the first person in history to come up with an elegant solution to the problem of the state, non-violent civil disobedience. Quit feeding the monster. For this Rothbard justly praises him. I do hope that you will read them both.

Previously published at http://www.lewrockwell.com

THE NEW SCIENCE OF POLITICS

A Review

2002

A reader suggested to me that my understanding of political government would be enhanced by reading Eric Voegelin's 1952 Walgreen lecture series published under this title*. I read the book.

There is no science in this book. The astrophysicist Andrew J. Galambos said, "Science consists of observables" (*Sic Itur ad Astra*, 1999). Professor Voeglin does not deal with observables, he deals with opinions. He criticizes the opinion of sociologist Max Weber about the nature of science, but he does not mention the seminal work on the subject by astrophysicist Sir Arthur Eddington (*Philosophy of Physical Science*, 1939). Voeglin apparently believed that a sociologist knew more about science than an authentic scientist; this kind of faith is the foundation of his book.

I find intellectual obfuscation objectionable, and Voegelin's discourse is nothing if not confusing and opaque to understanding. He would have us believe that the motivating principle behind politics is spiritual, and that the evolution of political systems depends on new developments in religion. This is to take Arnold Toynbee's opinion that dying civilizations bequeath their essence encapsulated in religion to a subsequent civilization, and set it in stone. Well, as Sportin' Life said, "It ain't necessarily so."

This is a professional academician at work. Voegelin offered one candid and honest remark (pg.64) about his profession: "The theorist need perhaps not be a paragon of virtue himself, but he must, at least, be capable of imaginative re-enactment of the experiences of which theory is an explication; and this faculty can be developed only under certain conditions such as inclination, an economic basis that will allow the investment of years of work into such studies, and a social environment which does not suppress a man when he engages in them." Never mind his misuse of the word theory, which in genuine science means a corroborated hypothesis, here he is validating the procedure of selective subjective speculation about the nature of reality as a tenured professor at public expense. I daresay that his liberal-arts audience got the message.

I suppose that sounds like sour grapes, but I have never envied tenured professors who must meet academic institutional expectations to keep their jobs, and who risk losing their entitlements by jumping fences. It is possible to study for a lifetime, and raise a family, on an ordinary job that leaves one free to think and to judge independently.

Voegelin did point out the remarkable similarity between mass faith in nationalism and mass faith in religion that takes us one step closer to understanding the efficacy of political propaganda, and for that I thank him. But he did not take the next step of comparing the rule by force and fraud, that is political government, with proprietary self-rule, that is economic government. This fence he could not jump, for it would have liquidated his job.

This book did not, in fact, enhance my understanding of political government, but it did enhance my understanding of the political philosophers who endorse this ancient and futile paradigm.

*University of Chicago Press, 1952, 1987. Available at www.amazon.com.

ON EDUCATION

2001

When I was growing up during the 1940s, a local independent service club brought a speaker to town every year. His name was Sam Campbell <http://www.samcampbell.f2s.com>. He gave a lecture on nature while his wife showed movies of animals and birds and natural habitats. Being a farm boy full of curiosity and little true knowledge about wildlife, I paid close attention to the pictures and the explanations.

Sam Campbell wrote a new book for children nearly every year and I always bought a copy. Then one year he had a new book (*Nature's Messages*, Rand McNally, NY, 1952) that he refused to sell to me. "This one's for adults," he said, "you are too young." Naturally I had to have that book right away. I badgered my mom for a loan until she bought it. Within, I found an intriguing reference to Henry David Thoreau's *Walden* <http://www.nanosft.com/walden/>.

The lady at the shop in town treated me like I was demented or pulling her leg when I tried to order the book, because I couldn't pronounce Thoreau correctly. I returned the next day with a piece of paper and I handed it to her. She had never heard of him either, but she agreed to order the book if I paid in advance. So I got my first copy of *Walden* at the age of eleven and my education began.

That Modern Library edition was an anthology of Thoreau's writing without annotation and it included such essays as *Walking*, *Life Without Principle*, and *Civil Disobedience*. I read *Walden* first. I wasn't so surprised about a grown man going off to live alone in the woods for two years, in fact I thought that might be a good idea, but I was surprised that a grown man would go through so much trouble to explain why. Grownups didn't explain why they did things, they just did them.

I should say that I did not understand at first that Thoreau had been writing this a century before I was reading it. I thought of him as an older cousin or an uncle whom I hadn't met as yet. I read him literally and in real time, as it were.

Thoreau was always asking difficult questions, something children like myself were not allowed to do. After a while I gathered that he did this deliberately both to think about an issue himself and to provoke the reader into thinking about the same issue. I did not experience this kind of attitude in school or at home and I kept this new approach to knowledge to myself. Some of his questions were so hard that I am still thinking about them fifty-years later.

From Thoreau I soon acquired the knack for asking questions myself. I discovered that if I was quiet about it, I could go upstairs into the adult library, a gift to the town from Andrew Carnegie, and I could look up answers in books I could not afford. If I found something important, I would save my money and buy the book. That's how I wound up reading *Voyage of the Beagle* <http://www.infidels.org/library/historical/charles _darwin/voyage_of_beagle/> before I was old enough to get a grownup library card.

My attitude toward knowledge was neither anticipated nor approved in provincial America during the fifties and it caused me a lot of grief in high school and later in college. Of course, it's all different these days! When I started having children of my own in the sixties, I worried for them. I didn't want them to grow up ignorant or restrained by ignorance, but I also didn't want them to pay a price for being curious and open-minded. It was a puzzle.

My wife and I discussed this problem at length and we made two decisions. One, get rid of the television set; two, read to the kids every day. That was the easy part. The hard part came when they grew up to school-age.

California had a law against home-schooling in the seventies or we would have done that. Our trial with a private "school" after kindergarten was disastrous financially and educationally; our oldest son nearly stopped reading. We were poor financially and we enrolled the boys in public "school" with great foreboding.

We were justified. Public "school" was an uphill battle each and every day for the next thirteen years, until each boy went to college on his own. Each and every day we had to undo the damage done that day by some "teacher" and then address the subject at hand. That took hours every day, after "school"; it became a full-time job. Some "teachers" we had to battle face to face, usually young ones who didn't know what they were doing, although sometimes older ones who knew exactly what they were doing. They called our boys "gifted" because they were always neat, clean, polite, punctual, and way ahead of their class. "Teachers" don't like "gifted" children—or their parents, especially the parents who come to talk to them.

The outcome was worth the effort. These young men went to college with faith in their own ability to think, to reason, to discover the truth, and with no faith in "teachers." If some assertion didn't make sense to them, they challenged it. Naturally they had trouble in required "liberal arts" classes, they knew they would in advance, but they did just fine in mathematics, physics, chemistry, and engineering classes, where "teachers" could not lie. Both graduated with honors and today both are busy recreating our world and getting rich in the process, which is the way things ought to be for everyone.

My education began by accident and I don't envy any kid who learns to think by accident. Our children must learn to think for themselves. The world of mankind is too intertwined and too precarious these days to have confidence in the intentions of successive generations of children who cannot think for themselves. "Schools" cannot be trusted to teach children how to think. Public "schools" have every incentive to teach children not to think, but to be obedient servants to their masters. Many private "schools" have the same mandated agenda. Home-schooling has the potential of teaching children how to think for themselves as long as the parents treat the official curricula with careful skepticism; not everything in the textbooks is true.

My own best hope for education is the Internet, where knowledge is quickly passed on to the curious. On the Internet, teachers can forgo their cradle of tenure and obedience and take their chances on real teaching; I mean, charge for their services with a money-back-guarantee of satisfaction.

This idea is catching on. You can almost hear the halls of ivy groan and crumble while the "teachers" cry out to the state for protection. The state is a protection racket. In part, in fact, this idea answers one of Thoreau's hard questions; when mankind grows up, we won't need the state at all. I think that education on the Internet can lead the way.

Previously published at http://www.lewrockwell.com

SNAKE CHARMER™

2001

A Snake Charmer™ is a shotgun. It's a cute little thing only twenty-eight and a half inches long, single shot, with a stainless steel barrel and a plastic grip. It takes a three-inch magnum .410 shell. That means, to those who don't know it, that the ammunition for this delightful shotgun (http://www.snake-charmer.net) is three-inches long and not quite a half-inch in diameter. When I moved across country, I left the one I had owned for twenty-years behind.

This was like parting with an old friend. If I had the talent, I would write an aria of farewell, like Colline singing goodbye to his old overcoat in *La Boheme*, for the truth is that I had purchased this shotgun from my best friend. Sad, leaving it like that, but necessary, or so I thought at the time.

I was sitting in my apartment in the heart of the coastal mountains of northern California studying road maps and thinking about what to take with me on this journey to Florida. I had narrowed it down to music, books, sculpture, and computer, but I had some odds and ends left over, including this shotgun. What should I do with it?

I've lived with guns in the house since I was a child. Dad kept a loaded .22 rifle and a 12-gauge shotgun leaning in a corner of the kitchen pantry, which was common practice among farmers in those days. He taught me how to fire that shotgun when I was seven, the same year he taught me how to drive the tractor. My brother, eight years older, had a regular gun closet in his bedroom with an assortment of pistols and rifles and shotguns that I envied. I used to carry his .22-short double-barreled derringer in my pocket when I was prowling around the countryside; I even took it to school with me once in the fourth grade for show-and-tell. Guns were part of everyday life in rural America during the 1940's and nobody thought anything about it.

Taking a gun along to college never occurred to me and several years passed before I bought one of my own. Pretty soon I owned a .22 revolver and a 30-30 rifle and my wife and I spent a couple of evenings every week out at the firing range, competing with each other. She always won. Then hard-times came and I sold them.

Later on we settled down in Santa Rosa, California, and we bought a house not far from the hospital where I worked. This was before the orchards that surrounded the city for miles were turned into subdivisions and I felt so safe that I used to walk to work at night. Sometimes we even forgot to lock the doors. We didn't own a gun.

Then one day the cops were chasing a car through town and the guy ditched it and started running through an old residential neighborhood, with the cops hot on his heels. The guy ran through the front door of one house, shot an old lady sitting there, ran out the back door, jumped the fence, ran through the back door of the next house, shot a young mother and child, ran out the front door and got away.

I read this front-page news story several times. The crazies had arrived. From the few crazies I had seen myself in the emergency room and from the stories I had heard about the new drugs on the streets, I guessed that we were entering a new era of risk and uncertainty. I decided to buy a gun.

I admit that the odds of surviving a surprise assault with a deadly weapon are mighty slim; that's why SWAT teams don't knock first at three a.m. Even if the old lady had been sitting in her rocking chair holding a loaded gun in her lap when the crazy ran through the door, she would probably not have had the time to fire it—but she might have. A locked screen door might have slowed the guy down long enough for her to wake up and grab a gun and fire it. Maybe. We'll never know, she didn't have a gun.

Dad couldn't see the use of having an unloaded gun zipped into a padded case and locked into a closet. I couldn't either. I mean, if you needed the thing, you needed it right now, not five minutes from now. I didn't want anything complicated either; I had some experience with jammed cartridges and stuck safety locks and I wasn't about to take it apart and oil it and put it back together every month so it would work if and when the time came. I'm not interested in playing around with a gun any more than I'm interested in playing around with claw-hammer, so I wanted a small-ish thing that could reliably pack a big wallop without a lot of fuss. I bought a gun catalog and I found the Snake Charmer™. It just happened that my friend had one to sell.

I took it to the firing range and I fired it a few times just to convince myself that it worked. My wife fired it too and once again proved that she was a better shot. We taught our kids how to load it and fire it. That's it. We didn't use up even one box of shells. After that it gathered dust under the bed or on top of a bookshelf for year after year, seldom cleaned, but loaded, ready, and waiting.

Now what should I do with it? I tried to figure the odds. I would be alone, driving for ten to twelve hours a day, with at least two gas stops and two pit stops per day, and a motel stop at the end of the day, for four days. My pickup could break down and strand me in the middle of nowhere anytime. I could be stopped for speeding or for a burned-out tail-light. Whom did I have to fear the most? Crazies or cops?

You may think that this is an easy question to answer, but to me it was not easy. I knew cops and crazies both from the environment of the emergency room, where unheard of drugs and good old four-point leather restraints and lots of professional hands are available. I've never had to deal with these people face to face, alone, on the street or in my home or while I'm driving. I tried to imagine various possibilities.

Several images came to mind. Cops had taken to carrying multiple weapons and wearing bullet-proof vests and black uniforms. The black uniforms bothered me. Why black? These were no longer the "boys in blue" who were there to protect us, these were the men in black who were there to threaten us. It reminded me of Nazi history. Then there were images of Ruby Ridge and Waco and of SWAT teams murdering innocent people in their sleep in Los Angeles. Then there was my close friend, gut-shot by a cop in a restaurant parking lot for no good reason at all. These images added up to one conclusion: cops are dangerous people.

Funny, none of the images that worried me turned out to be images of crazies. I think I can see them coming, for one thing, although they don't wear uniforms and I may be deluding myself. Manson was still in prison, the last I heard, although Hollywood wants to forgive him and run him for Senate, like some other evil people they adore. Be that as it may, in the end I decided to leave my shotgun behind and to take my chances with the crazies rather than take any chances with the cops.

Well, I made it to Florida without a hitch, although I had a bad moment there at an Arizona checkpoint on the taxway. The guy asked me if I was an American citizen in English so broken I could not understand him at first. I started laughing, you see, thinking of Heinlein novels, and the guy was reaching for his gun by the time I said, "Yes! I'm a tax-paying American citizen!" Okay, he was probably a rookie. God save us from rookies.

America is beautiful. We can drive freely across a continent and speak the same language everywhere, we can use the same currency for money, we can shop at nearly identical stores, and one motel or gas station is much like another. Neighborhoods too, the construction materials may differ, but the way we live throughout the country is much the same. Unfortunately, so are the crazies and the cops. I was kind of hoping there would be a difference.

One of the first stories I heard in Florida was about a crazy who randomly murdered people living near railroad tracks. I decided not to live near a railroad track. Recently I read about a cop killing an unarmed college kid during a routine traffic stop. Then I saw the local SWAT team proudly hailed on the evening news. Too much! It's just like California. So I'm back to square one, should I buy another gun?

Against the cops there is no defense. Zero. Zip. Don't even think about it. Cops have the legal monopoly on the use of deadly force and there is nothing we can do short of changing the nature of government itself. If the SWAT team hits the wrong address, we're dead meat. If a nervous rookie misinterprets our intentions, we're dead meat. But what about the crazies? What are the odds that a couple of crazies would run through an unlocked door during a dinner party and kill everybody in the house for fun, as a couple of crazies did in Kansas not so long ago? Would a little .410 loaded with one 00 buckshot shell make a difference?

Yes, well, now that I've thought it over again, I'm going to go out and buy myself a brand new Snake Charmer™. You just never know when you might need one.

Previously published at http://www.lewrockwell.com

The License

2001

The state does not license cats. Why is that? They license dogs, why not cats? Could it be that cats refuse to be licensed? Are they too independent, stubborn, stuck-up, wily, and disobedient to be licensed?

According to my dictionary, the main meanings of the word, license, are: *a. Official or legal permission to do or own a specified thing. b. Proof of permission granted, usually in the form of a document, card, plate, or tag.* I never knew a cat who ever asked anybody for permission to do anything, so maybe that's the answer.

But let's look at other categories of licensing. We have to license cars and trucks, but we do not have to license backhoes or lawn mowers. Does that make sense? Evidently the demand to license a thing is not inherent to the thing. I mean, these things all have engines and wheels and they move around, but we only license some of them. Why license cars? The individual car is already identified by the manufacturers' number, why do we need another one? The fee, of course, goes to support a state bureaucracy consisting of bored and indifferent individuals who are only working there for the wages and benefits and who couldn't care less about their career, if you can call it that. So why bother?

Yes, I know, the real reason we must license cars is so that the state can keep track of us. It's the same reason we must file a personal income tax return. Americans, unlike Europeans, have never been required to register with the police whenever they move from one place to another and we probably would not do it. This works.

What does a business license accomplish? Well, I guess it proves that you're seriously in business, although in most cities you can't be in business without one. So it's outright extortion, like property taxes, going to fund city government services that you didn't want anyway. Police? Well, maybe you do want police protection of your property, but police won't go near a riot and they're always too busy elsewhere, so you'll have to pay extra to hire your own.

How about a marriage license? That's something everybody really needs. How many times has a business asked you to show them your marriage license? What is this? Of course, in legal disputes it serves as a record of marriage, an implied contract, but what's to keep couples from making explicit contracts that could be used in private arbitration of disputes? It wouldn't be romantic, I suppose, but then waiting in line at the county clerk's desk isn't terribly romantic either. Neither is divorce court.

But we all know that doctors and dentists and nurses and such need to be licensed. Don't we? Their license is the state's guarantee that they are fully educated and competent at their business and that they won't cheat you or cause you bodily harm. Right? Okay, take away that guarantee, the state doesn't guarantee anything. But the license proves they're educated and competent, doesn't it? College degrees also prove they're educated and the validation of supervisors also proves they're competent. In fact, these are the very things that states use to issue the license. So what does the license prove? Why is it necessary? Why do we believe in it?

When I started working in hospitals back in the sixties, my particular niche in that world was not licensed. We had our own private organization that issued a certificate after a person voluntarily submitted to testing and that certificate was accepted in hospitals all over the country. Specific institutional education was not required to qualify for that test, but a person had to have two years of supervised experience and the endorsement of two of those supervisors to apply for it. That could get real sticky.

People who knew the business had to be convinced that you knew the business before they would commit themselves to endorsing you, and it was up to you to convince them. There were no textbooks on this subject in those days, but there were textbooks on anatomy, microbiology, physics, pharmacology, physiology, and chemistry; subjects that you were expected to know. There were also complex machines to learn inside-out, because you had to be able to fix them yourself if they broke down.

This was during the forging of a new profession, brought about by emerging technology. The doctors and the technicians were determined to find better ways to keep people alive after surgery or trauma, so the era of life-support machines was born. The technicians took their responsibility seriously, and they did not make entry into their world easy. People who just wanted a job could look elsewhere.

Of course, there are parasites in any business, no matter how much you try to get rid of them. When you have a national organization that supposedly represents thousands of people in a business, you necessarily have people running it. At first those people still worked in hospitals and ran the organization on the side, but the membership kept growing and the dues piled up and one day there was just too much work to be done at the office. The bureaucrats arrived.

Other things happened. Medicare refused to recognize the profession and all the Blues followed suit, which created a big reimbursement problem for hospitals. Hospital administration gradually became a profession too and adopted the model of organization from the government and the old rust-belt industries, the top-down pyramid, which required a department head who had to attend meetings instead of treating patients. Ambitious young doctors saw opportunity knocking and began to write research papers and textbooks on the new technology. Medical centers started formal in-house education programs. Voices were raised here and there demanding that we become genuine, validated, professionals, just like the doctors and the nurses, by asking the state to license us too.

I objected to that, naturally, and the national organization duly published my objection in their journal. I predicted that licensure would destroy the quality and the integrity of the practitioners and thus would destroy the credibility of the profession itself. This was not well received, particularly by those individuals who resented the threat of ostracism for inadequate work and the onerous difficulty of acquiring that piece of paper the way we had been doing it. They wanted schools. They wanted teachers who would be reasonable and understanding. They could get what they wanted if the state required graduation from a school to qualify for a license. From big empires do little empires grow.

I have heard it said that professional licensure came into existence at the insistence of professionals themselves who wished to restrict access to their field, the idea being to raise the price by limiting the supply for a given demand. I wonder, though, how much the cry for licensure was driven by simpler motives like envy, jealousy, and fear, like the motives behind the anti-trust lawsuit against Microsoft? I mean, if a person could demonstrate exceptional expertise in a field and contribute to innovation in that field, would it really matter to similar professionals if that person is licensed? I don't think so.

I would like to be able to say to my young and hopeful colleagues, once more, "I don't care where you learned it, just tell me how you would use the Henderson-Hasselbach equation in this situation," instead of depending on the license they acquired by graduating from a program and taking a multiple-choice test, thus satisfying the requirements of the state licensing board.

The structure of the licensure process in our society sits on a foundation that presumes there is some state authority that knows more than anybody else, that knows best who is qualified and who is not qualified to do something, without any guarantees. The fact that this authority is a person who merely collects and files documents demanded by a checklist prepared by a committee is totally ignored. None of these people are accountable in a malpractice lawsuit, for example, because they issued a license to somebody who was totally incompetent to do the licensed job, but who was fully competent to supply the required documents. Documents don't do surgery. I think we'd all be better off if we left the certifying of medical professionals to insurance underwriters who have a financial stake in being right. Insurance could guarantee to the consumer that the practitioner is educated and competent, the state cannot.

So let's consider licensing software engineers. Immediately one realizes that if Mr. Bill Gates had been forced to get a license first, the world would most likely not have a Microsoft Corporation today. We read about thousands of young people who renounce the tedium of higher education for the excitement of writing software, which they learned to do on their own, and creating their own Internet companies. Some succeed, some fail. I can just see some bureaucrat focusing myopically on the failures and saying, we ought to make it easier for them, their self-esteem depends on it, and I know how to give them all equal opportunity: license them! Make them all the same!

I do hope that I haven't given somebody an agenda in that paragraph, but here's another idea, the government could license writers too. Didn't the Soviet Union do something like that? This wouldn't be censorship, mind you, that would be unconstitutional, but no writer could be published who was not licensed, a wholly different matter. I wonder what committee would set the standards? Ah, the New York Times! I wonder about the rules a writer would have to obey? Education requirements, tests, continuing education, fees to be paid? A whole new bureaucracy devoted to ignoring complaints? And all paid for by the victims, just like the DMV and the state licensing boards.

Elegant idea, and many a politician would pant to dream of it, but it wouldn't work, for the same reason that licensing cats doesn't work. Not all people are as independent, stubborn, stuck up, wily, and disobedient as cats, but writers come pretty close, especially libertarian writers.

In the end, if we could just let go of our precious and profound co-dependent faith in the omniscience and omnipotence of the state, once reserved in our civilization for God alone, we might see that licensing professions is the codification of mediocrity. The most able and the least able are granted equality by the state, and the devil take the hindmost, who are us, the consumers. We pay for it. The license? Abolish it.

Previously published at http://www.lewrockwell.com

THE BOOMERS' WARS

2001

Back during the Clinton War on Bosnia, when our American pilots were bombing yet another Twentieth Century city into the Thirteenth Century, I wrote an angry little piece addressed to the American Baby Boomer generation. I seemed to recall that it was this generation that stood up to our Imperial War Machine during the Sixties and brought that war to a halt. In this war, however, I felt that they were strangely silent. I wondered if they had changed their minds about our Imperial wars in general? Or were they were hoping against hope that this monster they had put in office was not really the psychopath he appeared to be? I never could answer that question.

Today Clinton's War and Bush-the-First's War keep dragging on and on, as does the War on Drugs and the War on Dissenters, without much comment from the Boomers, yet this bulging block of population has reached its pinnacle of wealth and power and I suspect that it could put a stop to these wars too, if it wanted to. Because it doesn't, I conclude that it doesn't want to. Why?

The most obvious explanations that come to mind are that first the Boomers became preoccupied with their jobs and paying their mortgage and raising their kids and then suddenly realized that they are facing sixty and retirement, so they never took the time to think about what their government was doing. "Like, hey, man, we were, like, busy, you know." I don't think this answers the question.

The Boomers were born after the Hot War that we supposedly won and into the Cold War that threatened to annihilate mankind. As children they heard the local air-raid sirens blare and they peered skyward fearfully from beneath household furniture and schoolroom desks, waiting for the planes and the mushroom clouds. This was a common, everyday reality that I remember well.

While this particular practice came to an end, the threat of nuclear holocaust did not, which may have made these children wonder about the wisdom of their adults, and which children ought to still be wondering about today. Meanwhile, television came on the scene and filled every household with the inane antics of vaudeville and the new inanities of situation comedies juxtaposed with our glorious victories in old wars, the noble battles of new wars, cowboys and Indians, and the omnipresent threat of nuclear annihilation. Could this contradictory daily fare be called confusing?

With mature twenty-twenty hindsight today, many of us would agree that the American people were tricked into fighting every political war we have engaged in since 1776. The people don't want war, the politicians and the political bureaucrats and the war-material manufacturers want war. The people were either conned or forced into war by lies or bayonets. Vietnam was no different. I vividly recall a 1966 article in the National Geographic Magazine that depicted our compassionate Green Berets ministering to the peasants in Vietnam with nary a weapon in sight. See the good we do! Not quite the same picture we got from Lieutenant Calley a few years later. I don't know what kind of lies they were telling on television in those days, I refused to own one.

But the generation that President Johnson was sending to their deaths in Southeast Asia was much larger than he or his buddies could imagine and this generation was uniquely tired of all the lies inherent in the contradictions they had been fed. Money also played an enormous role in bringing the anti-war protest into every American home, for this generation had it. The government that could effectively shut up a Pete Seager's solo protest against the atomic bomb could not shut up the hundreds of minstrels who emerged to protest our war in Vietnam, minstrels who found a well-healed and ready market for their songs.

Even the mainstream media got the message after a while. The flower-children were not the misplaced waifs of their beloved Depression after all, they were the children of the affluent post-war middle-class and they did not want to die for nothing.

Of course, I will not forget to mention the cultural confusion also introduced by our space program, by the lamentable murders of the Kennedy brothers, both of whom should have lived to pay for their crimes, by the murder of Martin Luther King, and by The Pill. Each of these events would have had momentous cultural consequences if spread over decades; instead, they all happened in a compressed space of time. Then came the double-digit inflation to pay for our government's wars. It was too much to integrate. Gurus popped up everywhere to tell this generation what to think.

I honestly believe that if it had not been for the naïve dedication and hard work of a handful of college dropouts during the seventies, and the courage of their investors, our economy and world economies would have failed then and there, and precipitated the very Armageddon that everybody was expecting, the fiery victory of world socialism.

Children today cannot recapture this sense of a world without hope, although for inscrutable reasons of their own some are trying very hard, but their parents and their grandparents can. I wonder if this is why the old folks are silent while their government murders innocents in foreign lands, and militarized police murder innocents at home? Were these totalitarian Imperial values secretly buried in their hearts all along? Is this the world they wanted thirty-years ago?

I don't think so, but I am no longer sure. No, I am not calling for the old Hippies to rise up and publicly burn their AARP cards. No, I am not calling for the three-monkey RepubliCrats to make cloying speeches and then forge new chains for us behind closed doors. I am asking the Baby Boomers to wake up and look at the world they have created. Is this what you wanted? If it isn't, then speak out, and put a stop to these wars once and for all.

Previously published at http://www.lewrockwell.com

A Concrete Experience

2001

The California coastal mountains were uniformly brown and bone-dry when I boarded a plane bound for Florida. This was my first trip, my first exploration for a new home. I watched my first Atlantic sunrise the next morning as the plane approached the Jacksonville airport.

I also watched the ground and what I saw amazed me. Water. Lakes, rivers, and streams dotted the inland countryside. Green. All the landscape around the water was a deep, rich green. It looked wonderful to me.

Soon I was sitting outside in the fresh, cool morning, enfolded in the Florida humidity, and marveling at the green grass and the palm trees and the strange plants that looked like green swords sticking up every which way. Then I noticed something else. The power poles seemed to be made out of concrete.

My friend arrived and we drove into the central part of north Florida along broad, clean concrete highways cut through forests of tall green pines. Once again I was struck by the vibrant colors and all the waterways we crossed and, once again, by the huge concrete towers that carried the high-voltage power lines across the countryside.

The city, our destination, appeared to have been built right into the forest. Mature oaks and pines stood over mile after mile of homes in attractive subdivisions. Parked in the driveway at last, I got out and looked around at the picturesque park-like scene and then I noticed something else. The homes were all made out of concrete.

After living in California for thirty-five years, I had forgotten that people used brick and mortar and concrete-block for residential construction, because in California such houses would fall down. Florida is not threatened by big destructive earthquakes, however, only rare little tremblers, so these construction materials are safe to use. Moreover, the Florida homeowner can solve the serious problems of wood-eating insects and wood-rot in a humid climate by building with concrete. It makes good sense.

Concrete is also economical in Florida. The entire peninsula, once a seabed, is made out of limestone and sand, the chief ingredients of concrete. With the raw materials under foot and with the advantages of the product obvious to anyone who thinks about it, concrete is the choice building material in Florida. Maybe that's why the environmentalists want to put a stop to it.

I discovered the touchiness of this subject almost immediately. While driving around the county one afternoon, I came across a chain-link fence and a tall sandbank covered with grass that stretched for a half-mile or so along the road. Behind the bank rose new buildings and pristine smokestacks, but the place appeared to be abandoned. Miles from any town or even a noticeable habitation, I wondered what it could be? Asking about it later, I was briskly informed that it was a new cement plant, production halted by court order pending another environmental review. Curious, I discovered that a nearby city had approved this plant to boost its local economy in one of the poorest rural areas in Florida. Environmentalists in an adjacent city objected on the usual grounds of air pollution, water pollution, noise, and road maintenance expense to the taxpayer; that is, anything to keep the business in court and out of operation.

To enliven any table talk around here, all I have to do is ask about limestone mines or cement plants. It's like bringing up the redwoods in California. The response is the same. The analogy is also very close. Redwood trees grow naturally and very well in certain California environments, the coastal valley fog regions. Redwood lumber is both rot resistant and insect resistant, which makes it ideal for constructing earthquake resistant wood-frame houses. Most of the coastal redwoods were cut during the Nineteenth Century and used for houses in the San Francisco Bay area. They grew back. Today these dense forests are off-limits to the lumber industry and redwood is very expensive indeed in California. Concrete in Florida could be going the way of the redwoods.

Relatively cheap concrete products require two industrial operations, limestone mining and cement manufacturing. Moving concrete products requires roads and trucks. Environmentalists can easily attack production along any of these lines.

Since Florida is made out of limestone, mining it is an open-pit operation that takes up space and leaves holes in the ground. It's basically a matter of blasting the rock about once a month, digging it out, and then processing it. Environmentalists claim that the blasting is hard on local nerves and that it could disrupt the natural flow of water through the underground caverns. These caverns are otherwise well known for spontaneously collapsing and leaving big holes in the ground. The sinkholes are a reality, the diversion of water flow underground is a fantasy. Whether the blasting causes schizophrenia in local people, dogs, cats, raccoons, or manatees is never explicitly addressed.

Cement plants are supposedly the prime source of air and water pollution from dust, noise pollution from the noise, and traffic pollution from all the trucks coming and going. Not being deliberately stupid by any means, the people who own and operate these plants do not try to build them in urban centers, but tend to build them out in the middle of nowhere. True, there might be a river or lake or stream within three miles of the plant, that would not be remarkable in Florida, but three miles is still three miles, and people design these plants to pollute nothing outside of their own perimeter. Environmentalists ignore these small facts and focus on rust-belt models built up in their imaginations of what it might have been like a century ago.

The environmentalists I've met here in Florida also decry urban expansion. Down with the new subdivisions! It makes me worry about them. They speak these denunciations from inside a concrete house built within an old subdivision. Obvious contradictions aside, they evidently have made some kind of progress on their own terms. The new concrete plant sits idle and the new subdivisions are mostly wood-framed houses built on concrete perimeter foundations, the standard in California. Walls and roofs are a composite of wood chips and glue under the siding and shingles, guaranteed to rot out before any mortgage is paid off, although it will stand up in an earthquake. So what have the environmentalists accomplished here? I don't know, but hey, with this kind of logic, maybe I could sell concrete houses in California! I think I'd better call the Sierra Club in the morning.

Previously published at http://www.lewrockwell.com

LITERACY

2001

Recently I witnessed a shocking demonstration by a new, English speaking, college graduate. I don't normally talk about my writing with colleagues at work, there isn't time, but one intelligent youngster asked me a question that I could most easily answer by showing him one of my essays. He could not read it. I mean, he could sound out the words that he knew, skipping the words he didn't know, but he could not make sense of the sentences. After watching his ordeal for five painful minutes, I verbally gave him the message encoded in the English language that he could not read. He believes that he is educated, by the way, because he has a college degree.

This incident reminded me once again to stop taking things for granted. That reminder stimulated me to wonder how many people working in health-care are functionally illiterate? I can't find an answer to that question, but if it's so easy to slip through high-school English, the SAT, and the required undergraduate liberal arts classes without being able to read, then the probability that medical professionals can't read goes up.

I found a good article on the Internet called, *Illiteracy: An Incurable Disease or Education Malpractice?* http://www.nrrf.org/essay_Illiteracy.html#the-grimstatistics written by Robert W. Sweet, Jr., a former professional government education bureaucrat. Roughly a third of American adults are functionally illiterate, meaning they cannot read better than a third-grader, while government spending to combat illiteracy cost the taxpayers $463 billion between 1966 and 1996. Obviously, throwing money at the problem doesn't work.

Mr. Sweet explains that the problem began with a proposal by Horace Mann in 1837 to stop teaching reading by the phonetic method and to begin teaching reading by the "whole-word" memorization method. Mann's method didn't work, so it was adopted by teachers' colleges all over the country. Mann's method still doesn't work and it is still taught in teachers' colleges all over the country. There seems to be something stubbornly perverse about this.

I learned to read before I was sent to school. My step-mother's mother taught me, maybe by accident. She was a German-speaking cook with no education who liked to read bedtime stories to me. My favorite author was Thornton W. Burgess http://www.2020site.org/child_calendar/ and I liked his stories so much that I wanted to read them myself. Grandma made it a game. She would read to me, then I would read to her. It was great fun. My wife and I taught our own children to read by this same "method" using the same books. I do recall that the Mann method was used by the nuns in the first grade, the Dick and Jane nonsense, but I didn't pay attention to it because I could already read.

I think the whole argument about "method" is specious. Reading, like potty training, is more a matter of children copying the behavior of adults than it is a matter of teaching method. If children don't see adults reading, then how will they get the idea that reading is important to learn? Moreover, when children hear stories they like read to them from a book, then they will want to read the stories themselves. It is not method that matters, it is nurturing natural human curiosity that matters.

Presumably, this poses a problem for the children of illiterate parents, a problem that has excused massive government spending on remedies that haven't worked. That money came out of somebody's life and went into somebody else's life, while the unmotivated parents of unmotivated children remained unmotivated. It's just another con game, just another government racket, where only the bureaucrats win.

Mr. Sweet points out that the Mann method actually inhibits reading skill and he cites research to prove it. I don't know how this research is conducted, although it appears to be a trial and error procedure that permits total failure, something that is not permitted in medical research involving human beings. I think that research into learning reading skills ought to include parental incentive, i.e., I would not compare "methods" used in pubic schools, I would compare public school results with home school results and see what we may see.

Looking at literacy in the social context of television programming, reading is an utterly unnecessary skill. Serious content is delivered to the viewer in simple third-grade vocabulary, while violent content is delivered in non-verbal, primordial action. Judging by the popularity of this kind of programming, both literate and illiterate Americans tolerate it, I wonder if literacy even matters?

Literacy does matter to political governments. People need to be able to decode their written propaganda. People need to be able to decode their written indictments and the multitude of their laws, even if the people cannot understand them. A third-grade reading skill is critical to the perpetuation of this fraud, because if people could not read at third-grade level, the fraud would collapse. What if every defendant in every legal trial said, I didn't know that? I can't read!

But reading skills under political government must be limited. As Richard Mitchell writes in *The Graves of Academe* http://www.sourcetext.com /grammarian/graves-of-academe/09.htm the reading of unapproved books is forbidden in public schools, even if there were somebody left who could read them. An anonymous committee of people, who know nothing and who care for nothing except power in however a limited environment, choose the texts. To hell with Shakespeare then, "See Spot Run" is good enough for everybody.

Mr. Sweet writes that "the number of functionally illiterate adults is increasing by approximately two and one quarter million persons each year." Is this bad news? There are very few people who speak out against the imperial state and most of them do it in writing. What if they cannot be read? Do the functionally illiterate college graduates have any idea what is at stake in civil atrocities like Waco? Like Ruby Ridge? Like the War on Drugs? Like their local SWAT team? Do they have any idea what Slick Willie did? Do they know what "perjury" means?

If they don't, they will find out eventually, because they will be paying for it too. But two-thirds of American adults can read just fine. Two-thirds of American adults can figure out the stakes by reading the truth themselves. Tax-payers can stop the flow of their money into government literacy scams and let the illiterates learn to read if they want to. I'll do my part too. I'll give this essay to a certain college graduate and let him figure out the message for himself.

Previously published at http://www.lewrockwell.com

THE ELITE

2002

Political government is established among people to preserve and to protect the privileges of a powerful elite. Or as Butler Shaffer recently put it, http://www.lewrockwell.com/shaffer/shaffer26.html, "It should come as no great revelation to point out that democratically-constituted political systems have interests of their *own* that conflict with the wills of their alleged 'principals.'" Folks who believe that our current social situation, that is massive redistribution of wealth, massive debt, American Imperialism, and our growing police state, is a recent or expedient corruption of our federal Constitution need to read Murray Rothbard's *Conceived in Liberty*. The political elite was thriving in the 18th century as well. Richard D. Heffner described this issue succinctly in *A Documentary History of the United States* http://www.amazon.com/exec/obidos /tg/detail/-/0451628829/qid=1031079341/sr=1-2/ref=sr_1_2/104-32139 52-2639165?v=glance&s=books (pg.22), "...of the fifty-five delegates who participated in the deliberations of the [Constitutional] Convention most were substantial men of affairs personally interested in creating a strong central government." The common people, the colonists who had fought and won the war, were back on the farm, too busy to pay attention; of course, they weren't invited either.

True, they had to append a Bill Of Rights for the common people in order to gain ratification, but we have seen how quickly and easily that appendage is amputated when it suits the elite; in 1798, while the ink was drying on the Bill, Congress passed the Alien and Sedition Act, which made freedom of speech a crime.

The conflict between the political elite and the common people may be as old as mankind. Some have even elevated it to a quasi-natural law: that 80% of a population will be dominated by 20% at the top. I don't believe it is natural. I think it all depends on who makes the rules, and then enforces them. For example, on the issue of protectionism Murray Rothbard pointed out http://mises.org/fullarticle.asp?title=Protectionism &month=1 "that protectionism is out to mulct all of us for the benefit of a specially privileged, subsidized few—and an inefficient few at that: people who cannot make it in a free and unhampered market." A steel company can't do that, only a political government can do that, backed by armed force if necessary. This was one of several special-interest issues addressed by the elite writers of the Constitution, the regulation of commerce. I conclude that the 80/20 "rule" is an artifact imposed by the state, and is not a natural law at all.

Who are these people, the elite, and how many do they number? In terms of power, my own best guess would have to begin with the elite international consortium of bankers who own the Federal Reserve. Next would come the oil industry elite, followed by the automotive industry elite, the military-industrial complex elite, and the communication industry elite. Then the elite puppet politicians turn up, along with the legions of bureaucrats led by their own elite. There are maybe a few dozen people at the very top, with a grand total of around 56 million in the US (20% of the population, or 5% more people than voted for Bush II). One might say that this is a whopping big special-interest group! And, as always, they have the "lawful" use of force on their side.

This social system is manifestly unjust and unfair to the common people, the 80% who always pay for it with their lives in taxes, interest, inflation, and war. But is there a better way?

Imagine a cruise ship. This is private property that belongs to a company that will rent or lease space to you at a price agreed upon in advance. That space may be small or large, depending on the price, and it may include food and entertainment, depending on the price. The ship has a shopping mall, a supermarket, and a hospital, a police department, a fire department, a defense department, and an arbitration court, all privately owned. The company guarantees your safety and security, or your money back; no weasel wording appears in their contract with you, their customer. You may live there, work there, spend your lifetime there, if you choose.

Extrapolate from a cruise ship to a space vehicle with a population of six-million people. Or extrapolate to space-vehicle Earth. Certainly the risk to life, liberty, and property increases as the population increases, but if the vehicle is privately owned, no matter by how many people, and if individual security is guaranteed by contract with the owners, and the contract is insured, then political government by force and fraud becomes unnecessary and irrelevant, a mere footnote in the history of our Dark Ages.

And what happened to the elite of political privilege in this scenario? They're gone.

Previously published at http://www.lewrockwell.com

For the names of some of the elite, visit:

http://elitewatch.netfirms.com/

http://www.calneva.com/money/bilder99.htm

IF I RULED THE WORLD

By Robert Klassen

2002

If I wanted to rule the world, where would I begin? Foremost, I would want to control the money supply, for if I could control the money supply, then I would control whole governments, whole populations, and whole economies. I would not want to own them, mind you, for that would give me a bad name, but to control them still.

Let's say that four-hundred years ago a clever man earned a fortune in financing merchant ships and wholesaling imports. He made so much money that the King came to him and asked him to finance a war. This, he discovered, was a whole new way to make money, and where was the risk? The King would tax the people to pay him back, with interest to boot. Ah, but the King might lose his war, so the smart thing to do was to finance the King's enemy as well.

This clever man brought others into the business, then moved them to other Kingdoms, where they became bankers to merchants and Kings. These expanded the business even further and they became powerful people wherever they went.. They financed Kings and their wars, and they harvested the taxes from the people.

Then a newfangled thing came along, the American Revolution, and although there was no King on one side to promise to pay them, a committee of prominent people did promise to pay them, later, out of taxes. So they financed the war, but to be safe, they financed the King as well. The revolutionaries won their war, as we know, but they had not established a means to tax the people to pay for it. The bankers did not like that, so they pressed the leaders to change the rules, which they did with a brand new Constitution.

Naturally these people were no secret, for they were the leaders of society, but who could keep track of them generation after generation? Names change, after all, and some promising young man with an unpronounceable name might marry into the business, and allow it to grow in a new direction unknown to the people in general.

Some societies were easier to control than others, and the new republican forms of government sometimes spun out of control. People who believed that they were free and independent were particularly troublesome; unauthorized innovation could result in unimagined sources of wealth that could only be corralled with the greatest difficulty. Legislation was the solution, of course, but it always lagged behind new technology, and some of the wealth always got away—for a while.

The American Revolution was laid to rest easily, while the Industrial Revolution nearly escaped, but those who control the money always gain control of the rest in the end. Some bold and clever men saw that the key to controlling republican forms of government was a strong central bank that belonged to them. Impossible dream? The Federal Reserve Act was passed in 1913, and the US State became their own.

If I were the leader of this group, what would I want to do today? Corral innovation in information technology, and crush independent fledgling companies. Corral the Internet, and crush independent free flow of information. Entangle the whole population with rules and regulations and taxation, making true independence of thought and action nearly impossible for the common individual. Keep up the drumbeat of constant threats of war, terrorism, and financial failure to break the spirit of liberty and independence; strip that Bill Of Rights from the Constitution, and return it to its original intent. If I controlled the State, I would want the people to serve it, and to pay for it, diligently, and without complaint.

Whew! What a mad agenda! I am so glad that I only want to rule myself.

Previously published at http://www.lewrockwell.com

No Conceivable Reform

Alvin Lowi, Jr.

December 1999

I am keenly aware of my personal identity, a cherished gift from my parents. I would boast of my individuality as though it was a privilege were it not for the fact that all other people are similarly endowed. Yet, we are all different and in my case, I may celebrate my individuality more often than most. Thus, I have become known as an incorrigible individualist and I rather enjoy the distinction.

From my perspective, I observe a lot of anguish is being suffered among those people newly disillusioned over "the system," its injustices and absurdities. To them I say beware of all public plans and policies! More specifically, be aware that the "public" is a fictional entity. The only real entities are individual persons. The "public" is merely an excuse for a gang of ambitious political adventurers and exploiters to ride herd over others. It is an illusion that figures into all "government" mischief. How such an illusion came to pass is a story no less clever than The Wizard of Oz and a lot more factual.

The history of politics and its notions of "government" leads me to the conclusion that all political government is naked conquest and politics is but a scheme to subvert self-government and monopolize all "government" in the hands of an elite few. Self-government consists of self-discipline, and politics simply takes its cues from this fact and constructs a paternalistic Leviathan of regimentation over all in outrageous mimicry of the self-governing individual parent. This politics does as if it had the legitimate authority.

I set aside the word "government" here in quotes to indicate that the political version of government is irrelevant to if not destructive of real government. Real government is self-government else there is no government whatsoever. Without self-government, which is natural, government degenerates into a bunch of rackets. While rackets are natural, too, just like cancer, smallpox, syphilis, and AIDS, they tend to produce anarchy (no rule) resulting in social atrophy. Without a modicum of self-rule, society contracts and humanity declines inasmuch as the world can support few people without the benefactions of social processes such as exchange and specialization. Who cares? Certainly not the rulers who, come what may, expect to survive on the loot they can forage from whatever humanity is left.

Although the contest between the individual victim and the political state that is out to conquer him seems most poignant and grossly unfair, I resist the urge to engage in reform activity. I am a naturalist when it comes to humanity and society. Thus, I regard politics as an epidemic disease. As I see it, "public" health can be improved only as individual competence, initiative, and prudence are perfected, practiced and spread throughout the population. These traits are not only essential for making a life worthwhile but they also provide resistance to political infection. I observe that all people still alive have some grasp on such traits so that an expectation that they will exercise them from time to time and to some extent is not too unrealistic, provided they are not deluded by false promises of protection without effort.

Clearly, some level of social life is continuing notwithstanding the insults and assaults of political government. Such continuity is attributable to a residuum of individual initiative and responsibility. Paradoxically, the state is depending on a continuation of the same thing.

Looking at the political disease from this perspective, I suppose the most virulent "public" infection is the state monopoly of "public education." The compulsory, tax-supported institutions known mistakenly as "public schools" are where innocence, curiosity, critical thinking, and self-confidence are systematically stolen from the children in order to make them more docile subjects of the paternalistic system when and if they become adults. In the absence of educational alternatives that can effectively compete with the state's compulsory regimen, the indoctrination and brainwashing inflicted thereby will continue resulting in a lasting intellectual injury for most children. From this viewpoint, gun-run schools are a better accouterment to the state than the armed forces, the police, or the prisons. The seemingly intractable problems of statecraft are readily understandable when the true mission of the "public schools" is comprehended. That mission is first and foremost the perpetuation of the state. Good citizenship (read obedience and loyalty to the nation, right or wrong) takes precedence over all mere learning. In this campaign, the teachers' unions conspire with the bureaucrats to protect their exclusive franchise for the convenience of the state.

However, I am optimistic about the natural inclinations of people when they are sober, i.e., not intoxicated by illusion, delusion, bemusion, and confusion. I observe that in a strictly private and confidential encounter, most people who have no status in the system other than citizenship, will sober up for the duration of their seclusion. A few will remain so and live by the courage of their own convictions thereafter. How they may reconcile their intrinsic and indispensable selfhood as they grapple with their superstitions regarding citizenship is a curiosity for me and, no doubt, a concern for them.

It is well known that the banana that leaves the bunch is generally skinned and eaten. But what of a bunch of undifferentiated individuals? Their lives are not their own, which is contrary to their natures. In such a collective, normal, innocent human life becomes furtive, perhaps even subversive. Submerged in the collective, the individual is a guaranteed victim no less at risk of free-lance criminality than he would be as a solitary human. Apart from the collective, the naked individual human has a chance of survival in the presence of some feral Homo Sapiens. His chances improve in proportion to his prudence, knowledge, and skill. State protection is an utter illusion. Ask any of the multitude of its victims.

I belong to no group other than my family and humanity as a whole. This "membership" I inherited. Thus, politics has no relevance to any of my legitimate concerns. Therefore, there is nothing for me to *Do* with or about politics but to understand its pathological consequences, which persuades me toward studious abstention. I try to avoid letting my nose be counted in any political poll whatever lest I inadvertently sanction a continuation of the political process that threatens my existence.

While there is no way to avoid exposure to political propaganda, I rejoice in not being compelled to participate in plebiscitary activities. Reclaiming the time I would have otherwise spent at the polls agonizing over ridiculous choices among false alternatives leaves me time to study more significant phenomena and practice more fruitful activities. For example, when I discovered that over 80% of the mass media menu consists of political hash, I found I could readily live on a no-hash diet. By excluding political hash from my diet, I awakened to find I was saving myself a lot of time and anguish. Substantially relieved of these constraints and burdens, I was able to attend to matters more [central] to my life, which greatly improved my sense of well-being. More and more, I was able to ignore irrelevant "information" and concentrate on more significant (for me) but less "newsworthy" data. It was a great comfort to discover I could make such judgments on my own recognizance without the benefit of journalistic "assistance."

In France, the media is known as the "Fourth Estate," and it is becoming recognized in this country as the fourth branch of government. No wonder, then, that the media thrives on the status quo or threats to it. Actually, it is the status quo that is the enemy of the people. So in a real sense, the mass media is a big part of the "government" problem. This explains my delight in discovering the internet phenomenon growing as a competing source of information, served up by and accessible to individuals without obligations to sources or regimentations of interest.

Inform yourself and speak your own mind!

You have nothing to lose but your chains.

Previously published at http://members.aol.com/vlntryst/wn101.html#ncr and http://www.non-voters.org/noreform.shtml

---

The Utopian

2001

Many writers complain about and criticize the state, including me. We all seem to be suggesting that if only we can arouse the people, then we might turn things around. That seldom happens. The real problem lies in human nature. For example, the people are themselves often the secondary beneficiaries of the looting state. While they may sympathize with our call for free-markets and an end to war and taxes, nearly every person is dependent on the state for one thing or another, and is not about to give up his or her personal benefits for the larger good of mankind. That this socialist economic system is on the verge of total collapse means no more than the personal knowledge that this body will die some day, an existential denial that is critical to continuing life itself, and is part and parcel of human nature. Thus people may see a calamity approaching without acknowledging that it means anything to them personally.

My own thesis is that the use of force to get what we want is too deeply imbedded in our animal nature to acknowledge, and thus we tacitly approve of force in certain consciously defined circumstances, such as war. However, the Industrial Revolution has provided us with tools of war unimagined to the political philosophers who gave us the political governments that wield these tools today. Now we have the tools to destroy mankind in the hands of the very worst kinds of men, democratically

152

elected mediocrities, men without principles. This is more than just a dangerous situation, it is species extinction waiting to happen.

Our dilemma is that people cannot face the consequences of the use of force at the same time that people tacitly approve of the use of force to get their own way. This is exactly the same blindness regarding the tacit approval of wanton looting and redistribution of wealth by the state out of the personal self-interest of citizens. This is to say that man naturally tends to be a violent and self-centered creature in certain circumstances. The plain fact is, man cannot change the nature of man, but man can change the nature of his institutions, maybe before it's too late.

We could create human institutions designed to eliminate the efficacious use of force and fraud throughout the habitations of mankind. We could create and advertise and sell non-coercive systems of justice and security to the people in open competition with the state, products so efficacious, so cheap, and so guaranteed that people can't resist buying them. I want to live a world where I can buy insurance against the risks of force and fraud, that is, coercion, not only by individual defectors from the Golden Rule, but also by political government itself.

I am accused of being hopelessly utopian with this proposal. The very idea seems unnatural somehow. It is. We could curb those natural tendencies among human beings that have brought us to the brink of extinction, although the means to do so appears to be unnatural. We could eliminate that institutional expression of natural human tendencies we call the state. I don't believe this idea is any more utopian than learning to fly is utopian (and unnatural), but I am utopian in this respect, I cannot do it myself. I cannot write the programs or create the networks or found the companies, because I am a technical ignoramus and I am nobody's entrepreneur; I believe somebody else could do the job better than I could. I can only write criticisms of the state, and suggest that there might be a better way to provide security and justice without coercion (see http://www.nugvdigm.com). Is that utopian?

Jacket Endorsement

Social philosopher Spencer Heath maintained that we can t recognize atrocity for what it is until we can entertain an alternative. The example he gave was chattel slavery in the ancient world; few questioned it and fewer still raised their voice against it. Having already outlined the natural alternative to political (i.e. tax-based) government in his companion book, *Economic Government*, Klassen now articulates with rare clarity why political government is atrocity.

He calls this book "the end of my foray into criticism of political government." I welcome this implied emphasis on the health of society rather than its pathology. But if articulation of the pathology is called for, Klassen has done it with skill and clarity, dispassionately, and with forbearance.

Connoisseurs of political behavior will deepen their understanding and strengthen their analytical skill when they recognize that the subject of their study is social pathology and they themselves are pathologists; for a pathologist can only understand his subject matter in the light of social health. That is the contribution of this book and its companion book, *Economic Government*.

Spencer H. MacCallum, social anthropologist and author of *The Art of Community*.

0-595-25811-5